Mainly Mo[...]

*Dedicated to Mary Anne and [...]
as without their mutual co-o[...]
would not have ma[...]*

£1.50

A SOCIAL HISTORY STUDY FROM 1906 to 1930
WITH A DIFFERENCE

The facts in this book are all true but to protect the identities of individual characters and their relations, names in some cases have been altered.

12 Beaconsfield Rd, 1909
L to R Mother, Author,
Auntie and Daughter,
Sisters Ada and Hilda

Published by
Sewardstone (E4) Investments Ltd.,
Hague House,
Sewardstone Road,
Waltham Abbey,
Essex EN9 1NB.

Printed by
The Woodgrange Press Ltd.,
98 Woodgrange Road,
Forest Gate,
London E7 0EW.

October 1986

ISBN 0 9511832 0 6 (Softback)
ISBN 0 9511832 1 4 (Hardback)

All photographs copyright and permission must be obtained before reproducing.

CONTENTS

LIST OF ILLUSTRATIONS		iv
ACKNOWLEDGEMENTS		v
FOREWORD		vii
PREFACE		viii
INTRODUCTION		ix
CHAPTER 1	Beaconsfield Road	1
CHAPTER 2	Chelmsford Road	16
CHAPTER 3	Byfield Road	24
CHAPTER 4	The First Wedding	35
CHAPTER 5	School Days	41
CHAPTER 6	Trams	57
CHAPTER 7	A Unique Journey	62
CHAPTER 8	Entertainment	71
CHAPTER 9	The High Street	81
CHAPTER 10	The Initial Post	92
CHAPTER 11	The Building Trade	96
CHAPTER 12	The Halls of Pleasure	112
CHAPTER 13	An Imaginary Stroll	122
CONCLUSION		133

LIST OF ILLUSTRATIONS

Page i	Frontispiece
Page 3	Winnie, Harold and May.
Page 11	Archie, George and the author Harold.
Page 12	A London Street Orderly generally known as Scavenger Boys.
Page 18	Mother and Father taken at rear of 42 Chelmsford Road in 1914.
Page 21	(Top) Boston Road Peace Party 1919. (Foot) Mr Murfet, coal merchant.
Page 26	G. J. Walker on Salisbury Plain, 1915.
Page 34	The dog that ran sideways when drunk.
Page 37	Bride and Groom – Fred and Ada.
Page 43	Gamuel Road Infants School 1910 Christmas Play.
Page 47	Mr Wood the expert rubber thrower, with the author and school Head.
Page 53	Frank Murfet – The all important school "character".
Page 54	The George Monoux School Labour Certificate No. 1.
Page 64	Driver of Sheen with author and family group.
Page 66	A facsimile of Grandmother's stone box mangle.
Page 101	Snowey Bradds and some of his handiwork.
Page 107	The author helping with Mann Crossmans Sports Pavilion construction.
Page 111	The author on a Builders outing – 1924.
Page 119	Stanley Rollings, light heavyweight boxer – 1922.
Page 121	The author and family group at Margate – 1926.
Page 130	Wall's Ice Cream tricyclist on Portsmouth Road – 1930.

ACKNOWLEDGEMENTS

My sincere thanks to the following persons and organisations for their assistance and their personal efforts which helped me in my research. With apologies to anyone who may have inadvertently been omitted.

Mrs. Leslie Blundell, B.A., A.L.A., Librarian to the Borough of Waltham Forest and

Mr. John James, Editor of *Waltham Forest Guardian*, both of whom gave encouragement and help for which I shall be ever grateful.

Mrs. Jean Welby of Waltham Abbey, who typed relentlessly and gave unstinting assistance.

Mrs. Doreen Williams of Waltham Abbey, who assisted Jean whenever possible.

Councillor Tony Simmonds of Chingford, Past Mayor of Waltham Forest.

Susan Ashworth, Mrs. Arlott and John Evans of Vestry House Museum.

Mr. Tony Burton of Waltham Abbey.

Mr. Frank Murfett of Bognor Regis.

Mary Clayden of Sawbridgeworth Council.

Mrs. Theobald, Hon. Sec. of "The Evergreen Club" Sawbridgeworth.

Mr. Robert Hill of "Liverpool Victoria Friendly Society".

Mrs. Lilian Hickey of Eastbourne.

Mrs. Mary Harvey of Southend.

Mr. Springett of MacMullen's Brewery, Hertford.

The staff of the following libraries and museums:
Waltham Forest
Waltham Abbey
Loughton
Enfield
Guildhall, London
York Museum
Institute of Agricultural History, Reading.

Cartoons by Phil Gascoign.
        W. F. G. Walker

FOREWORD

This book is the conclusion of 10 years research. It is a local history book with a difference, worrying less about dates and spotlighting the characters existing in the area earlier this century.

The descriptions bring alive the happy and the sadder moments of one man's earlier years.

I have been pleased to be associated with the book's preparation in the last three years. The writer's enthusiasm and remarkable memory mean there are many pearls in the book.

He has so much information, that the writer could have continued typing his memories effortlessly for some time. This book, then, would never have been completed. A follow-up book to use the excess of material would almost certainly be as interesting as *Mainly Memories*.

By
John M. James,
Editor, *Waltham Forest Guardian*.

PREFACE

By Mrs. L. Blundell, B.A., A.L.A.
Librarian and Art Council Officer to
The Borough of Waltham Forest

MY first contact with Harold Walker came when he sought my opinion about the first draft of his then untitled reminiscences of pre-war Walthamstow. Since then I have watched the book's progress from early draft to final publication with great interest.

Born in the then urban district of Walthamstow in November 1906, the author spent the early years of his long life there before moving to Waltham Abbey during the Second World War. *Mainly Memories* recounts his recollections of his childhood and early manhood, primarily in urban Walthamstow but also in the more rural Sawbridgeworth and Wareside to which he was a frequent visitor.

Schooldays, street scenes, domestic life, early employment in the building trade and service with the local fire volunteers are lovingly described to create a fascinating picture of a pre-war world which has long since vanished.

Today, the author lives in Waltham Abbey with his wife and is still actively involved in the family insurance brokers which he founded.

Mainly Memories is not merely a book of recollections. The author has put a great deal of effort into researching the background to the events and institutions described. As a result, it should appeal not only to the general reader but also to the more serious student of local and social history.

INTRODUCTION

IT is not uncommon today for many famous and infamous persons to portray their life story. Politicians, criminals, actors, even various individuals who endeavour to play a guitar, in an attitude of self abuse, have all been involved. In some cases murderers have not been exempt. Apart from a "Band of Hope" certificate (since dishonoured) and an uncollected wartime medal, I cannot claim any further distinction. Nevertheless, I find great pleasure in describing social history in the form of nostalgic memories. I trust you will find the same!

The family of Haines consisted of four girls and two boys. In seniority was George, followed by Alice, my mother Mary, Jim, Sarah and Ada. They became motherless, by the birth of the last named. George also died early of TB. My grandmother's premature death was commonly accepted as "the will of God" in that period. An ailing father, known colloquially as "Swab", had experienced the apprenticeship and horrors of being a boy sweep.* By sheer effort, he had become one of the organised body of master sweeps, who championed the use of the new invention.† This organisation opposed those who flaunted the vague laws, which were intended to protect boys and *girls* from this appalling practice. Petty fines and ridiculously short prison sentences were proving useless. His second marriage to a large and strict taskmaster, resulted in the four girls leaving for domestic service as soon as possible. In later life they settled in Walthamstow and Leytonstone.

My father was a journeyman plasterer, whose parents I never met. Mother was a strict thrifty God-fearing person, with Victorian ideals, and rather frightening to our friends at first sight, but mellowing later. She could be garrulously humourous, especially in women's company, and sometimes suggestive. Her affection, although at times evident, was strangely guarded. She met father while in service (to a lord) at Broadstairs, he working on the property at the time. He must have been successful in overcoming her reserved nature, he being her complete opposite. He lacked a sense of responsibilities, but had a cheerful carefree disposition, which increased when indulging in his occasional drinking sprees. He shared this with a weakness for gee-gees, and smoked, as well as chewed a choking shag. His idiosyncrasies are disclosed among other peculiar characters, as the pages are turned.

The abolition of boy sweeps was finally successful through the magnificent effort of Lord Shaftsbury in 1875. For years deaths of boys and girls from the age of five had often occurred. One terrible example occurred in 1875 whilst a boy of eleven was retrieved from the boiler flues of Fulbourne Hospital, Cambridge, in spite of the resident doctor clearing the mouth of the exhausted child "of soot and stuff" and administering brandy whilst the victim was in a bath, the boy died. These inhuman happenings were commonplace. William Wyler, the master sweep, received six months hard labour for this offence and the boy was registered as the last victim of this nefarious practice. Further studies are portrayed in K. H. Strange's book "The Climbing Boy".

†*Chimney Brush.*

CHAPTER 1

Beaconsfield Road

I FIRST saw the interior of a Warners flat in Hove Avenue, Walthamstow, on a typical foggy morning on 26th November, 1906. My only reaction to this momentous event was an ear splitting yell. Mother had been in labour from the evening before and during the night had implored father to "fetch the doctor". Father, in his fuddled repose, assured her not to worry. "It" would arrive in the morning, as all the others had. After an interlude of seven years I had appeared on the scene, completing a family of seven. This comprised two brothers, aged seven and nine, and four sisters, aged between 11 and 16. Welcome or not, I had come to stay. After my intrusion into the family and the lapse of time, a move was in the offing. During the ceremony of "The Churching of Women" at St. Saviour's, Markhouse Road, mother was informed of a likely residence, by another mother, also receiving the Blessing of the Lord, via His pale faced, sonorous representative.

Number 12 Beaconsfield Road was a terraced, two-bedroomed house, with the front door opening directly into the parlour, commonly termed "the front room", following through to the kitchen. Stairs between the two rooms led to a minute landing and two bedrooms on opposite sides.

How a house, or shall I say a cottage, of such meagre proportions housed a family of seven children and their parents in a clean and quite respectable manner, I shall never know.

The problem was greatly eased when my four sisters reached school-leaving age and were quickly ushered out to "service", leaving a surplus of oxygen for the rest of the family.

This character-studded road has long since disappeared under the so-called modernisation schemes, superseded by the characterless monstrosities devised by so-called planners.

I recall it as a cosy, friendly thoroughfare – a sandy road, populated by the most interesting friendly people, who all depended on Bobby Beckham, owner of the corner shop, for their meagre purchases of provisions.

We all imagined him as a bloated capitalist. Poor man, his working hours were endless, opening at 6am. Whatever time he closed, an erstwhile customer would not be content until he or she had disturbed his well-earned respite, by knocking at the door interspersed by loud taps on the window, for some forgotten purchase, with little advantage to him (e.g. profit on one pound of sugar at that time was one farthing).

All this was accompanied by the noise of children, including myself, indulging in horseplay, throwing stones at the enamel advertisements for "Hudson's Soap', "Rova Cocoa" and "Lux" conveniently fixed on the side wall.

The firewood bundles stacked in front of the counter were the easiest items to steal. In the corner was a paraffin tank, operated by a hand pump, placed near unwrapped loaves.

Hidden from view was the bacon slicer, a fascinating piece of recently acquired modern machinery, which needed us to crane our necks to make sure we received a fair weight. Thus the mixed aroma was, in a word, delicious.

The 7lbs jars of pickles and jams stood handy. I often saw Mr Beckham stirring these containers very vigorously to conceal the mildew persistently forming on the surface. For these delicacies, you took a cup. This was first weighed before your order was ladled out with a wooden spoon.

The Wares were the elite of the street. Mrs Ware made full use of her aitches, adding some at intervals, then leaving a few out to compensate.

The Brents were very religious, although painfully poor. On one very special occasion I was permitted to stay for tea, after playing in the garden, generally termed "the yard". Four of us were breathless and excited, seated on a wooden form, probably a gift from the local chapel, eating one huge hunk of bread and margarine each. Even at home we had jam and reasonable cut slices but, in contrast, I was perplexed to observe my friend Johnny's elder sister, who provided part of the family income, seated at the end of the table in a chair – a place of honour – and had a 1d tin of bloater paste for her own delight. She was obviously a privileged person. Mother and father presided on the opposite side. He was served a real bloater and was seated in a Windsor armchair. In the eyes of the family he was "all highest". A short, thick set man, he had no personality or distinguishing features except he was permanently clad in a heavy corduroy suit, a porter-like hat and sported a badge on his coat indicating he was an employee of the Lea Bridge Road Water Board.

Later in life I met Johnny, who had become very dedicated to chapel life. He implored me to hear a missionary speak at Keswick Mission Hall. I met him, quite innocently, at the top of Beaconsfield Road and was most embarrassed, if not surprised, to find I was one of a "jolly band of pilgrims" and found myself marching to the chapel accompanied by a concertina enthusiast, extolling the virtues of themselves and singing "Come and join us".

Left to right: Winnie, Harold and May.

While having every regard for the happy band, I must admit it was not particularly my mode of life. I was more reserved in my beliefs and attitudes towards religion. However, here I was being ushered into a pew, handed a hymn book and joining the rest of the congregation in "Gospel Bells". Then came a fiery exortation from an evangelist, *not* a missionary as I had been led to expect.

This fiery gentleman would have put Billy Graham to shame, or at least relegated him to the second division of that profession. The beginning of his oration was quite a normal sermon. Later, though, the advocate of the Lord developed into a resounding cry to "all sinners to come forward and be saved". This appeal was accompanied by the organ, whispering soft music, and the lights being slowly dimmed as a spotlight suddenly focussed on the star performer. A brilliant piece of theatre. His exultations from the pulpit created a wave of hysteria among some, a mute look from others. Sadly or otherwise, my reaction was complete embarrassment. Ironically, this particular chapel provided my first job in 1924 as a plasterer, which was one reason why I had agreed to accompany Johnny so that I could survey my handiwork of previous years. Some were affected by the atmosphere, while I remained mute. Finally, the tirade came to a conclusion and poor Johnny turned to me with great emotion and enquired if I was "all right with God". I could only gasp "Yes, thanks" and make my escape with as much decorum as possible. Later it occurred to me, why did not Johnny advance to be saved. Then on reflection, it dawned on me, he was!

Further along the road were the Smiths, a pathetic family, with four boys and one girl. They were fathered by a small, dark man with a drooping moustache, which obscured his mouth. His lower lip was only seen when it protruded to suck the dripping nodules of whatever beverage he had imbibed in. The mother was of gigantic proportions, with a greasy complexion, surmounted by a pair of black protruding eyes. On her upper lip was a straggerly black moustache which, while not as profuse as her husband's, had offshoots on various parts of the face. Her arms showed an awful red rash and sores, possibly a type of excema. Her boisterous bust and mountainous stomach were supported by extra large feet, encased in male boots for shopping, and carpet slippers for home use. I cannot describe her legs as these, in common with the period, were not generally exposed. When rarely seen abroad she sported her husband's cap, which only partly concealed her mousey unkempt hair. When this lady who, incidentally, had a pleasant manner, opened her front door, a peculiar smell exuded from the interior stinging the nostrils of visitors. When invited to enter the abode, I made every excuse not to. At times when it was necessary, I resorted to chewing my cap, which tasted far better than the aroma which floated around, and even invaded the palate. So why visit the Smiths? At home, I was usually presented with two or three large jars of cod liver oil and malt. It was awful stuff, with at least 75 per cent pure cod liver oil and no artificial flavouring, only fish. I was always thankful and relieved to give this concoction to the Smiths. At intervals, they would ask, "Have you any more of that treacle?" The family enjoyed it on bread!

Referring to this medicine, let me digress. I was, at times, taken to Saint Bartholomews Hospital for various childhood complaints or for my mother to apply for spectacles. My mother appeared to enjoy these trips, the walk from Liverpool Street, window shopping, plus the gossip while waiting to see the consultant. The garrulous ladies continued their endless discussion, during a further wait, on the hard forms in the odour filled dispensary. These seats, highly polished by countless bottoms, made lovely slides for the bored children. The climax came when I had to see a surgeon, whom I feared, probably because of my mother's subservient attitude to him and almost anyone in a professional capacity. This was due, no doubt, to her earlier life as a domestic, and rural childhood. I was fascinated by the reflecting circular mirror worn on the doctors head band, used for peering down patients throats, or any other orifice, offered for inspection. We were later pedantically informed "A tonsillectomy was necessary". We discovered later, via a severe sister, "I was to have my tonsils removed".

For this event I had to fast from lunchtime the day before the operation, except for a large dose of castor oil in the evening. It was necessary to rise at 6am in order to catch the 7.30am workmen's train to Liverpool Street, then the usual walk to Barts, except on this occasion, with a churning stomach. Money could not be wasted on fares! Even my most exciting thrill of watching the London Orderlies* generally called Scavenger Boys risking life and limb and at times succeeding, failed to interest me. On arrival all the

---

*The Scavenger Boys employed by the City of London, their correct title being "Orderly Boys" numbered two hundred. I found little has been recorded of their history.

The Guildhall Library proved a helpful source of reference. An original photo showing the subject with his tools of trade was obtained.

I personally witnessed these cheerful types, scurrying among the traffic, diving under the heads of moving horses and miraculously avoiding faster traffic with fascinating skill. The refuse collected by them was mainly manure, scooped up by their razor edged dust pan. The pan would be swivelled with lightning rapidity and skill, the contents then dumped in roadside iron bins.

These were cleared at night by the regular dustmen. I have no statistics of the accident or fatality rate, although it must have been high. It was a common site to see a small crowd gathered round a pale faced victim who had recently been involved in an accident.

When a quick recovery from shock was made, he would return to duty with the typical cheeky smile. A permanent disablement resulted in a pension of 10/- per week. It is to be assumed these extremely agile and dextrous cleaners were disbanded following the increase of motor traffic.

"victims" for the surgeon were herded into a room with screens, which had one direct entrance to the operating theatre.

Eventually, "Walker" was called and I drifted towards the open door. On entering the theatre, I saw the previous patient being wheeled out horizontally with blood trickling from his mouth. I walked into the theatre unaccompanied and was immediately taken aback. The surgeon, showing complete unconcern, told me to "jump up there, sonny", with an inclination of his head towards the operating table. He was lecturing his eager students, on a piece of bloody flesh, adhering to his forceps, which without the flesh, were terrifying enough. This may have been of interest to them, but certainly not to me. A rubber mask was placed over my face, accompanied by a sweet choking odour. Then oblivion. My next recollection was a nightmare of being caught in a huge spinning wheel with a loose strap attached that kept slapping my face on each revolution. My eyes cleared to view a row of bloody-faced children laying on mattresses on the floor, with a probationer slapping my face intent on reviving me. A grim-faced sister clapped her hands and remonstrated "Mothers: come on, get your children dressed and hurry please". Everyone, as usual in those days, did as they were told. We were ushered out imperiously in a state of confusion. I was walked to Liverpool Street for the Walthamstow-bound train with a further walk home. Then bed, feeling absolutely dreadful. All this in one day meant only one thing, you had to be tough, then. After care, as outpatient, brought the glorifying gossip for mothers, meeting her counterparts, repeating the polishing of benches. The finale, took us to the unmistakable brown tiled dispensary, to collect "the treacle", which ultimately finished up on the bread of the poor Smiths.

At various times, my mother would receive odd left-over clothing and shoes from the employers of sister Ada, who was "in service" to Mr and Mrs Scholtocks of Howard Road, then a high class residential area, which many respected, and viewed with awe. The employers welcomed my parents, sometimes accompanied by myself, during school holidays. I would see my parent doing a day's washing for 2s 6d a day, which included travelling time. The journey was at least two miles each way. It was a glorious day for me, playing in the garden, gazing at the huge silver dish covers displayed on the wall, while partaking of wafer thin bread liberally spread with rich yellow butter. Whatever was left after my mother had sorted the gifts from the rich man's wardrobe were given to the Smiths, necessitating further calls, and so enabling me to inhale the ozone again, which issued from their abode.

The Smiths' daughter, Hilda, was an exceptionally pretty girl. Not so her eldest brother, George. He had an enormous head, two large protruding eyes, a pendulous lower lip and the expression of a harmless, though mentally retarded man. He had the posture of a gorilla due to his bent knock knees and shambled rather than walked. His long swinging arms, added to this sad spectacle. He always opened the door, presenting a prepossessing figure, to any unprepared caller. Another family member was Arthur, considerably older than me, but in the same class at school. On one occasion he was requested to accompany a sick boy home. This was a common occurrence. Some pupils had eaten no breakfast, while others, in fear of punishment if late, only half digested what had been eaten. Arthur returned agog with excitement: "Coo, old Alexander 'aint arf rich. You should see his house. He's richer than you." Such were his comparisons, it was a surprise for me to learn my family were rich. We were unaware of it.

Next was Charlie, almost as retarded as George, but not malformed. The fourth and eldest had an extremely kind nature but, again, was handicapped. He had a leg which swung outwards in an arc, while the foot met the ground at right angles to its opposite number. He, poor soul, worked for a greengrocer and walked beside his donkey hawking wares. If you can imagine his right hand coming up smartly and being placed behind his right ear in an endeavour to give added power to his shouts of "cabbage, potatoes, pot herbs, fine ripe cherries", this, coupled with the lame leg, created a spectacle rarely seen.

Next door to us was a large unique family, too numerous to know exactly how many. Rather than costermongers, they were more like high class gipsies, yearning for the open air and giving unusual care to their horse.

After unharnessing the horse the cart would be left in the front garden. The family would then parade Dobbin through the parlour and kitchen, cleverly manoeuvre it into the scullery, to introduce it to the back garden. On very cold nights Dobbin often remained in the flag stone scullery. Even for this thoughtful family, it must have been a little irksome being awakened by the horse stamping its hooves, and giving vent to its flatulence, through the night. Later, a shed was built.

The family preferred their evening meal alfresco, with a stewpot in true gipsy fashion perched over a fire on a tripod in the garden. "More wa'er 'Arry" was often heard when tea was being served after a meal or when the beetroots were being boiled in preparation for sale the next day. "More wa'er 'Arry", became a family colloquialism. On one occasion, sister Ada was generously given this nutritious vegetable wrapped in newsprint. She returned indoors to throw it on the fire in disgust. Such was her opinion of our illustrious neighbours.

Sunday in Beaconsfield Road was full of interest. It was no day of rest, but a hive of activity and a pleasant change to the humdrum happenings of weekdays.

The delivery of the *News of the World* gave my father exceptional pleasure. He would sit in a high-backed Windsor armchair, which had a hard cushion to conveniently hide out-of-date periodicals, such as *Pearsons Weekly*, *Tit Bits* and *Answers*. After his weekend luxury breakfast of kippers or bloater, bought from Daines smoke hole in Gamuel Road, he would sit back and endeavour to choke us with the smoke from his cherrywood pipe, filled with "Nut Brown Best Shag".

The kitchener was permanently alight, being the only means for cooking and supplying hot water. The large blackened iron kettle, was always seen steaming on the hob.

Whether requested or not we were all beguiled with snippets of news from Dadda. Any gruesome murder, would be related with relish.

One particular Monday morning, he bought the *Chronicle*, looking for any plasterers vacancies. He was unemployed again. Then came the astounding news: "The Titanic had foundered"*.

Had war been declared overnight, none of us could have been more bewildered. Just a brief note had been published in the stop press. Later that day, the cry of "Extra, extra, Titanic disaster, read all about it!" was heard on the streets by enterprising news vendors. Later still came the horrific news of the many drowned, this brought back sad memories to father.

I was only six years old at the time, yet such important incidents remain vivid in my mind. Especially the cry of the news-boys. Wireless and television may have hastened news, but has killed the exciting cry of "Extra"! This unexpected news affected father a great deal. It was a reminder of a tragedy that had haunted him since boyhood. In the early morning of September 3rd, 1876, he arose agog with excitement with the expectation of the day to come, it being his twelfth birthday. His pleasure turned to horror on finding his father dead and partly burned in the living room of their home. The unfortunate man has arrived home very late and had fallen asleep by the fire and later succumbed to a heart attack. It was on this very day father, with his parents, had prepared an excursion on the favourite Thames Pleasure Steamer "The Princess Alice". This popular ship left Swan Pier, near London Bridge, that morning bound for Sheerness. There were approximately seven hundred passengers on board, including a fair percentage of

---

*The Titanic hit an iceberg just before midnight on Sunday, April 14, 1912 and sank at 2.20am on April 15, with 1,512 people losing their lives through inadequate saving apparatus. The inquiry which followed resulted in enforced boat drill by all crew and passengers on all sailings, a 24-hour radio watch and adequate space and sufficient boats for all passengers and crew.

children, all on pleasure bent. After a happy day the ship was approaching the bend in the river on its return journey in the gathering dusk. Preparations for docking were being made, the band had packed their instruments. First class passengers had returned to their cabins to collect their belongings, families had gathered in small groups. It was near Woolwich in the gathering gloom that the lights of an iron collier "The Bywell Castle" was seen bearing down on "The Princess Alice". Captain Grinstead gave the order to "Warch his helm" with the expectation the oncoming ship would alter course to port. The expectation was not realised. "The Bywell Castle" struck the ill-fated vessel amidships on the portside, cutting it almost in half. In less than five minutes the "Princess Alice" had sunk in deep water with the appalling loss of between 550 and 650 souls, including Captain Grinstead. Many bodies recovered were unclaimed and buried in a mass grave in Woolwich Cemetery. The rest had been carried away by the relentless flow of the Thames or trapped in the saloon. At the prolonged inquest it was disclosed the ship was licensed to carry 936 passengers. Its life saving equipment consisted of two lifeboats and twelve lifebuoys. Mother, with her fervent religious tendency, referred to father's possible escape as "Divine Intervention". Father always declared, although drink contributed in some measure to his own father's death, that he could not reconcile that the collosal loss of life had been ordained to save his own miserable one.

The "Bywell Castle" mysteriously sank without trace with no survivors five years later in the vicinity of the Bay of Biscay. The lack of life saving equipment was noted and rectified on pleasure ships in the Thames and yet not 36 years later the same negligent omission occurred on the "Titantic".

Sunday mornings were most exciting with many callers. The milkman came on his second round, having left our pint in a gun metal can with its brass handle supplemented by an elaborate triangular brass hinge at 6am. His second call heralded by a singing cry of "Milko" in a variety of keys was to collect his weekly account, an indication that the customer had proved reliable over the years. If not, daily payment was demanded.

Invariably there was a heated discussion on the amount to be paid and memories on both sides needed jogging. The mistake was not always that of the harassed "Milkie", as he was popularly known, but when in later years I was employed as a schoolboy assistant, it was not unknown to find his small income being supplemented by a little manipulation of both milk measure and book-keeping.

His three-wheeled cart, which he pushed, had an enormous milk churn with highly polished brass fittings. He would further carry a 2½ gallon milk can to the door in case a further supply was needed. This nourishing liquid of to-day in some cases then harboured TB Bacilli[†], a frightening scourge of the time.

Next interruption came from the newspaper man, collecting his 2d for the Sunday paper. This was the only newspaper delivered to our house. I was always fascinated by his dog-eared little notebook, with its red cover, and his minute stub of indelible pencil, constantly wetted by the tongue, causing his mouth and surround to take on the appearance of an ancient Briton starting to paint himself with woad.

Then came the hawkers. There were no Sunday trading laws to impede their progress in life. Private enterprise was growing.

My favourite was a shabby and rather dour person, who was a little surly, arriving with a bundle of what appeared to be newspapers. He sold comics and would cry "Coloured comic" in a monotonous low-key grunt. Sometimes, if my father was in a generous mood, I obtained one. My father, anyway, secretly read them himself, in an assumed detached manner.

The colourful comics came from America and in no way resembled those published in England. Similar comics still supplement today's American bulky newspapers, in which news is secondary.

The winkle and shrimp barrow, with its attendant, toured the streets before positioning itself outside the Duke of Cambridge public house. In charge was a tall, stooping man, with a fearsome cast in his eye and a head that swayed from side to side as if looking for some obscure object. Housewives were cajoled by him to "splash out" for Sunday tea, which used to be almost as important as Sunday lunch, or dinner, its more commonplace title.

His arrival was always accompanied by the cry "penny wink", interpreted by all to indicate that winkles could be bought for 1d per pint. Father in his teasing manner affirmed that this man was enquiring "where's Win", and added rather thoughtlessly, "He's looking for you Win". Winnie's reaction would be to hide behind mother, while in turn father would be upbraided by mother with a partly concealed smile.

My weekend treat was to accompany my father to the tiny barber's saloon, situated in a private house in Boundary Road, where I could feast my eyes on the English, but extremely tattered, variety of comics (see *A Stroll in 1912* chapter).

[†]Tuberculosis, known as "the white scourge", was prevalent and in most cases terminal: in 1944 with the introduction of streptomycin and other drugs, a cure was found at last.

Left to right: Archie, George and the author Harold.

Whatever the family's financial state of affairs, Sunday dinner was sacrosanct, even if it meant the front room clock having to be pawned, which sometimes occurred. That involved my father walking to the pawnshop in High Road, Leyton. There were "pop shops" nearer, but previous experience had proved a larger cash advance and better terms could be obtained in the High Road. Competition existed even among pawnshops.

The midday repast over, the rest of the family, Winnie, Arch and George, were hustled off to Sunday School. I, being too young at the time, was allowed to stay at home, spending most of my time in winter looking out of the front room window for the muffin man, listening for the clang of his hand bell.

Eventually he would appear, with his tray of muffins perched on his head, covered with a waterproof material plus a green baize cover. He was far too cunning to lose his voice, in the winter fog, by calling out his wares. Everyone knew what his bell meant. How I longed to sample that mysterious commodity. No! Either by prejudice, or economy, mother when asked, would comment, "He keeps them under the bed" or "They are carried on his head". Saveloys, faggots, jellied eels, were all considered unhygienic, thus considered forbidden fruit.

The arrival of sisters Ada and May, allowed out from their place of service, graciously permitted each fortnight, contributed to a special treat for all to be present at Sunday tea, after which we repaired to the front room.

This sanctum with four hard leather seat open back chairs, plus one horse hair sofa, equally hard, a bamboo table, in the centre, on which was placed a twisted brass columned oil lamp casting a warm, if not low glow. This was enhanced by the reflection in the mirror fixed in the overmantle.

The "watnot" stood like a sentry in the corner, while on the two low cupboards either side of the fireplace were a collection of school prizes, plus the Holy Bible. The mantlepiece itself was cluttered with photos and ornaments, the latter advertising the fact that they were 'a present from Southend and other far away places'. The centrepiece, a clock (still in my possession) which permanently registered the incorrect time.

Turkey red highly polished oil-cloth covered the tiny room, except that part in front of the fireplace (which was seldom lit). Here was the result of the family's effort, a home made rag rug, a dust collector of all times. A small bamboo table graced the window from which hung a 2/11¾d pair of lace curtains, held back by a pair of brass curtain bands, mother's prized acquisition, religiously polished weekly.

A mahogany work box, inlaid with pieces of mother of pearl, stood on the table, holding among a motley of paraphernalia a well worn pack of playing cards, one of which was often found to be missing and usually discovered by mother, who had an uncanny knack of finding any "lost" article.

Her remarks "I must take those curtains down" or "This ceiling needs whitewashing, George", etc., were commonplace and always inferred "something had to be done". The evenings were generally spent by gossip of the events or playing Ludo, Snakes and Ladders, and cards, not forgetting "Cod-em"*. We were, at that time, fortunately or not, devoid of a piano or music of any kind, until we acquired a gramophone, by way of a gift, this stupendous event took place through the good offices of "Uncle Jim Crabbe" a neighbour of our previous residence. This generous man was married to a Dutch Lady, whose English was extremely broken. His occupation was that of a cowman to a Walthamstow farm. Yes that's how rural Walthamstow was in 1912!

Mrs. Crabbe would often remark to mother, if her husband had imbibed, not wisely, but too well that: 'Shim is a proper pucker' (her j sounded as sh, whilst her b's sounded as p's). To me he was a great favourite, especially when he passed on his ancient gramophone and a number of brown half size, almost unbreakable one sided cardboard based records. I have since seen the replica of this now valuable antique machine in York Museum. It is an extremely rare model, the acquisition of this astounding invention, stood in pride of place on one of the low cupboards and transformed my life. At first I firmly believed, as I was informed by father, that a little man was inside the mysterious box who was responsible for all the entertainment.

Mother returned home from one of her regular visits to Mrs. Crabbe, who regrettably could not pronounce her newly-acquired name. When asked to state her name, she replied "Mrs. Crapp sir"!

We were informed that poor "Shim" had caught a tick from the cows, by not covering his head when milking. This horrible insect had infected him, resulting in a form of maggots under the skin.

Mother's highly coloured description, that "maggots were falling out of his head", was horrifying to all. Mother's descriptive exaggerations on various subjects were always startling.

She convinced me if I swallowed pips, the respective tree would grow in

---

*The game "Cod-em", equal number of players on opposite sides of the table. Captain of one side strikes a farthing on the table as a sign for his team to dive their hand under same. The farthing changed hands and on the command "Cod-em" the team raise clenched fists on the table. Opposite team can say away, to any fist with an endeavour to discover hidden coin. If discovered coin changes sides.
  Wins are marked up, first to reach ten wins.
  Squeels of laughter always ensued while hands were under the table, especially when courting couples participated.

my stomach. Likewise, if I cried at all "I would get water on the brain!" Whatever that may be.

Her thoughtlessness was brought to a sudden halt, when I started school as an innocent infant. I imparted to her lurid details of the conduct of the teacher, possibly with slight imagination, when recounting these events, while my parent was busily engaged in household chores. She would, without thinking, remark "I'll see your teacher and give her a good hiding". At one time saying in her usual way "I'll come and chop her head off" or "I'll give her bossiks"[†]. The following mornings I would repeat these lurid threats word for word to my long suffering pince-nezed, harassed female instructor, who in her high necked laced collar blouse, and wide belted, long skirt would survey me with horror. The continuance of these blood curdling messages, were at last brought to the notice of the head teacher, who in turn interviewed mother on the subject.

Mother's consternation can be easily imagined. With cunning and quick thought, she replied as coolly but not without some embarrassment, that her neighbour had been responsible by advising "Tell your mother to –" whatever had been said. Whether believed or not, the farce was brought to a close.

We have digressed from Sunday at No. 12 and can only add, summer time had an addition to the hawkers in the shape of Jack the Italian ice cream vendor, whose barrow with two tubs containing ice cream in one, and a plain white sweet concoction called "Ice" in the other. Nowadays ice enjoys the more glamorous title of "Sorbet". The latter of course cannot now be bought at the price then of ¼d per cone. He parked for quite a while in each street, introducing colour and luxury. The colour being his highly decorated barrow with scenes of sunny Italy, and a canopy with its gay stripes. The luxury of course was a weekly taste of hand churned home-made ice cream, a laborious job, that is now a forgotten art. Darkness was falling on a cold February evening early in 1914. We had retrieved the brass oil lamp, from the "front room", whose light was supplemented by the flames of the open range fire in the kitchen. I had completed counting the bobbles on the fringe of the mantle piece cover, and had given up trying to envisage the Thames Iron Works! Father always referred to the sound of the German Alarm Clock as such. I took a last lingering look at our sparse garden at the end of which stood a very large Pear Tree, which I almost worshipped. Beyond this was open waste ground. This ill fated tree was never allowed to father its abundant crop of Pears. When small and half grown, these hard samples were "Scrumped" by

---

[†]Bossiks, an expression unique to her vocabulary (meaning a good hiding) likewise "Skerrick" meaning nothing, "I have not got a skerrick". Have these peculiar phrases any origin?

the miscreants of my old school and consumed with the same abandon as the spoils of the "Great Bakehouse Robbery" mentioned latter. We move on the morrow! And snow is in the offing.

A London Street Orderly generally known as Scavenger Boys.

CHAPTER 2

Chelmsford Road

EVENTUALLY, the move to Chelmsford Road arrived. It was early in the fatal year 1914. Hilleries covered waggon was summoned, and the contents of our humble household were exposed to gawping neighbours. I excitedly assisted in transporting many articles by a coster barrow, that had to be specially protected, such as the watnot, wooden coal scuttle complete with highly polished brass shovel. This prize possession was never used for coal. It mainly held periodicals and music sheets, etc. Archie being seven years older was in charge and, as usual, teased me intensely. Chelmsford Road consisted of a motley range of houses, some quite respectable in my eyes, while others were in a deplorable state of repair, some unfit for habitation and consequently empty. A whole row of these were in evidence as we trundled round the corner. It was at one of these derelict hovels Archie halted the barrow and stated "this was our new home". My feelings of desperation and shock were evident and tears came to my eyes. Relief came later, on being reassured such was not the case and eventually No. 42, a rather better looking end of terrace cottage, was ours.

Chelmsford Road lacked the character and friendly atmosphere of our previous abode, but it was a degree above Beaconsfield, with one important exception, we had occasional visits of rats. These creatures were common-place. My mother with Mrs. Eaton, a dear old neighbour, were one day, as usual, gossiping over the garden fence and while engaged were distracted by a series of scraping and rattling inside the stench pipe, which ran up the side of the house. After a while they were astounded at the sight of a huge sewer rat emerging from the top, which was well above the gutter. It cooly surveyed the surrounding scene with obvious interest, and gave a casual glance at the two ladies below. It is not necessary to add that this definitely curtailed the morning gossip very abruptly. However much one may think this feat by the rat in question as rather improbable, the fact is it did this circus act to the consternation of both Mrs. Walker and Eaton, who disappeared as if by magic accompanied by female screams – this was no mouse!

An outstanding event of unique interest happened during our residence, concerning another neighbour, a Mrs. Manners. She had bouts of inebriation and, while under the influence, would emerge from the front door and create a disturbance by abusing all and sundry. This contributed much to the amusement of those who were aware of her failings, and the perplexity of those who were not. On one of these occasions, while creating a fracas and generally being a nuisance, two policemen appeared who had obviously been called, and began to quietly talk to her, and sympathise with her problems. They were so kind and considerate she was reduced to tears, and became quite maudlin, but at the same time began to pour out her tale of woe. The bobbies lent the most sympathetic ear and suggested she came into the street to tell them more "as it was difficult to hear her" and also confidentially mentioned, "She did not want everyone to know her business, did she dear". While pursuing this kind of co-operative understanding, Mrs. Manners fell for the five card trick by opening the gate and stepping onto the public footpath. Hey presto! She was immediately collared by the cunning arm of the law and most unceremoniously taken by each elbow and almost carried off to the police station while being garbed in a coarse apron and carpet slippers. The latter kept leaving her feet every few yards, and being monotonously recovered by one of the enterprising bobbies. It was a most ungracious ending to her open-air performance which curtailed the like happening for some time. These surely were the times when policemen were respected and law and order was strictly enforced. In this particular case, it was a case of a sobering night in the cell, plus a five shilling fine on the morrow at Stratford Police Court, with magistrate Jarman presiding. The only other event of any great significance was the declaration of war on Germany in 1914!

At the top of the road was a large area of open scrubland known as the boundary fields – actually the boundary between Walthamstow and Leyton. On the Leyton side stood the drill hall of the Territorial Regiment. Later in the 20s the Savoy Cinema was erected near the site. These "week-end" soldiers, as they were disparagingly termed, were suddenly all important, and were the forerunners of Kitchener's "contemptible army". The vision of these enthusiastic volunteers, clad in full kit, with fixed bayonets, glittering menacingly – filled every one with excitement. The glow of pride increased on the appearance of the regimental band who took the lead with the strains of "Colonel Bogey". As they marched away, very few could have had any knowledge of the carnage to follow. It was all going to be so easy, almost a holiday, "Over by Christmas at least". The South African war had only terminated just over a decade ago, the interval was over, the second act was about to begin.

Fevers, Diphtheria, T.B. in all forms were commonplace. It was not an unusual sight to see a victim of spinal, or certain bone diseases requiring complete rest, to be wheeled in a horizontal position, on a long wicker-work bed with protective sides, commonly called an invalid carriage. The patient was often left outside the residence, when weather permitted, receiving piteous glances from passersby. A motor or horse drawn ambulance was often

Mother and father taken at the rear of 42 Chelmsford Road in 1914.

seen collecting a fever stricken patient, while neighbours looked on anxiously from a safe distance. On these occasions we would hurry by the said ambulance superstitiously saying "touch collar, never swaller, never get the fever". This piece of doggeral was accompanied by touching ones collar, followed by spitting with a firm belief. One had waylaid the chances of being contaminated. The origin of this piece of superstition would be interesting to know.

Characters in Chelmsford Road were far fewer than Beaconsfield Road, apart from the besotted wretch, Mrs. Manners, whose ignominious arrest helped to break the monotony. There was a Mr. Daines, a rosy-faced portly man, with a charming manner, who was often seen wheeling his massive highly decorated wheelbarrow, while wearing a blue and white butchers' apron, crying, in a single monotone "Mee Mee". He held the shafts in a perpendicular position, while the iron shod wooden spoked wheel crunched along the gritty road, in unison with his extraordinary large boots. This contraption was laden with lumps of obnoxious smelling horse flesh, a delicacy for "Moggies" which, in turn, trailed around joining in his cry.

It portrayed a scene reminiscent of the Pied Piper of Hamelin, the pussies miraculously escaping the danger of the solitary wheel that revolved relentlessly. Slices of this tempting flesh were cut up on a bloody, fly-infested board placed between the shafts, by a fearsome looking knife. Portions were then spiked on wooden skewers, and placed in letter boxes or under the door knockers. Sometimes an enterprising feline was successful in purloining the tasty sample left under the door knocker. A brother of Mr. Daines, living in Gamuel Road, possessed a large, covered yard at the side of his house, complete with smoke hole. Here the most delicious kippers, bloaters and haddocks were prepared and sold direct from the greasy iron rods that festooned his unique shop. No planning permission, and certainly no objection from his neighbours, even though the effluvious atmosphere from the smoke hole could be high on occasions. His delicious end product was worth it all. When hawking his fish, his familiar cry was "all early" to be interpreted as (all oily).

Adjacent to Chelmsford Road was Boston Road, an interesting side turning boasting of a parade of versatile shops. The first was an empty premises awaiting a daunting tenant's speculative acumen. Next a butcher, displaying a meagre stock of meat with a few strings of mottled sausages, hanging forlorn. This picture always appeared the same. A bloody block with an attendant cleaver was a vivid reminder of Anne Boleyn's fatal demise.

Behind the white marble counters, supporting china and brass scales, with a pile of newspapers at the side, for wrapping purposes, stood the wielder of the cleaver. A gaunt heavy moustached man wearing a long rough cloth dark blue coat, a common apparel for butchers of the period. The sawdust strewn floor with liberal splatters of blood, was evident. The walls of the shop were of grained matchboarding which had gathered a fair coating of grease over the years, from the countless carcases, that had been hung. Nearby was an odiferous emporium, termed as a "Rag and Bone shop". This enterprise exuded a choking smell, resulting from the stock of metal, bones, rags, paper, jam jars, and every sort of rubbish, all of which were sorted daily. Nothing was thrown away by the populace, if it could realise a few coppers in this lumber palace. This type of shop has now disappeared entirely.

Next in line to add to the many and varied aromas was a wet and dried fish shop. The unsold wet fish was fried at midday and again from about 5pm to midnight. Billowing clouds of steam flowed from the top of the windows. The bare boarded floor was again smothered in sawdust and a high green counter, restricted the young to see over. This meant they clamoured around the lower flap at the end enabling a view of the roaring furnaces and, more importantly, being seen as well as heard. The coal was conveniently scattered on the floor, under a bench, on which the fish was prepared for frying. When stocks of fuel ran low buckets of coal were conveyed from the rear and tipped carelessly, enabling the dust to rise, adding a separate flavour to the fish. It was with fascination I watched the fryer, slapping the prepared portions of skate, plaice or whatever in a bowl of thick yellow substance, generally known as batter. When the fish was battered, in both senses of the word, and dropped into the boiling oil, or dripping, we were rewarded with a resounding crackle accompanied by the fryer wielding his wire tray with delicate expertise.

This was one of the errands I enjoyed – in fact, looked forward to. It was exciting to see the fryer open his two small furnaces to replenish the fire. One gazed at the blaze, imagining it was the stoke room of a liner or hades and feeling the heat hit your face, before facing the winter blast outside. It always seemed winter when fish suppers were on the menu. While serving the many customers, it was seldom the shop was not full, with the kids at the far end creating an incessant demand. The harassed server was at the receiving end of a constant verbal barrage of "two pen'orth and Middle Skate" or "tuppeny and a pen'orth" or "ha'pth of crackling" – the latter being exactly what it was, just fried up pieces of batter. Whatever the request, it always ended in "please" and was called as one would chant the psalms, except it was incessant. The din came mainly from the junior section, who unfairly were always kept waiting. The harassed server eventually dispatched the noisy mob, only to be replaced by newcomers, with even louder requests. This scene was surmounted by the pale glow that only gaslight can give. It shone

Boston Road peace party 1919.

Mr. Murfet, coal merchant, Boston Road.

like a beacon in the dark street, reminding one of a lighthouse signalling a haven for the hungry and cold.

The sweetshop was the next in line, which among its exciting stock, sold "lucky dips". These were a piece of toffee about the size of an old penny, stuck to the end of a small stick and placed in a triangular paper bag holding a smattering of sherbert. They were offered for your own selection and should you pick one with the toffee coloured brown, instead of pale cream, the reward was a stick of rock. This gamble cost one farthing so it needs no imagination to envisage how many prizes were contained in the box displayed. I, for one, can never remember being a lucky winner!

The window displayed little saucers of various attractions, such as "Bulls Eyes", "Hundreds and Thousands", honeycomb, locust beans, the latter complete with maggots, and a horrible tasting stick which was known as liquorish – not the black variety, but an actual greeny-looking branch or root of a plant. It had a horrible taste, and after being chewed resembled shreds of wood. It could not reasonably be fully masticated. Strangely enough children still bought it. I wonder what has happened to this mysterious delight?

The price of various sweets displayed in saucers was with a scrap of card on which showed 4oz per penny, or 2oz per penny, the latter bringing whistles of disbelief. The next was a general store reminiscent of Bobby Beckams, which has been previously described. A laundry followed, where father's weekly collar and dickey was laundered for 2d. This was the only type of neckware he ever wore, whilst out, and ripped off as soon as he entered home.

The last of the parade was the linen draper's, whose prices were not completely rounded off. They always finished with a farthing, e.g. one pair of curtains 1/11¾d. This cunning ploy was so that when anyone bought an article, the proprietor feigned difficulty in securing a farthing change, and passed over a packet of pins in lieu, thus making another sale. A point worth noting is that this little parade of businesses kept strictly to their particular calling and never encroached on fellow shopkeepers' stock in trade. It is so commonplace to-day, for example, to enter a butchers, and be contemplated by the accusing eyes of a cod as you turn away from the meat counter.

The first established family of coal merchants in Walthamstow namely Murfetts, operated from this road. Photos of his father and other studies were presented by his surviving, successful son, Frank, aged 80, now residing in Bognor Regis.

The Labour Certificate which permitted one to leave school before fourteen, was probably the last of its kind to be issued. The photostat of his school character is a document we, as schoolboys, all individually feared to lose. The threat of this being withheld if we proved unworthy hung over our heads like the Sword of Damocles.

The fact Frank became a J.P. and pilot instructor in World War Two is no discredit for the successes of many Gamuel Road pupils. I wonder if the photo of the 1918 peace party contains some one who is, or was, near and dear, to any erstwhile reader.

The damp conditions of our house and occasional visitation of rats finally caused the decision of my parents to move from this not too desirable residence. The constant odour of dry rot, arising in our tiny parlour, was reminiscent of an open grave. An excellent crop of fungus was always evident. Father's usual facetious remark "That we could speculate in growing mushrooms" did not amuse mother, who was determined to seek a more salubrious residence.

CHAPTER 3

14 Byfield Road

DURING the early part of the 1914/18 war, we again moved to the address above. We had become a little more affluent, which was also occuring to some who had escaped the fighting services. As a result of this terrible conflict, business stirred, and full employment became inevitable.

No Hilleries covered waggon this time! A "Presslands" pantechnicon instead, drawn by a pair of magnificent carthorses, with two "real" removal men. Instead of assisting with a hired costermongers barrow (at 2d per hour) I experienced the thrill of a ride on the tailboard, which had been left down, exposing our now improved home, including a new "front room" suite. This consisted of one hard green sofa, with an even harder bolster, it was stuffed with horse hair, that at times escaped in single hairs through the fabric. There were four, hard leather seated chairs with the most uncomfortable backs, which in co-operation with the highly polished seats, were successful in causing one the inclination to slide off. By way of a change, it was a relief to stand up.

The new residence, was a distinct improvement, although its rent was higher. This was approved by mother who remarked to father, as she observed the pattern tiled front path, "it's worth the extra sixpence, George, to see the nice path". The ease to throw a pail of water to clean same was obvious to her, as previously there had been a broken strip of concrete, that had defied her efforts in household pride. To me it was the ultimate! Yes we were certainly moving up in the world, for the price of sixpence. It was an intimate little road of only 24 terraced houses, inhabited by a reserved type of persons. Unfortunately our pride and pleasure was short lived! Having moved in late winter, we found as spring approached we were not the only tenants. There was another large family who began to reveal themselves. They came out of hibernation as warmer weather arrived, and were delighted with our company in bed. You may have guessed it – Bugs!

These filthy vermin were a source of terror to all, especially the female members of our family. Relentless war was waged on these obnoxious creatures. There were no council exterminators employed, and actually no really efficient patent killer. Sulphur candles – doubtful insecticides, even painting the beds with paraffin, plus extreme cleanliness finally overcame these insidious parasites, although mother and three of the sisters were appalled at this catastrophe. The least perturbed was father, whose facetious advice to get rid of these "steamtugs", as he termed them, was not appreciated by the female element. His suggestion to "paint one blue, so the others would think he was a copper and bugger off" was not considered amusing. Another suggestion, of a cruder nature, was to "wait until one excreted and then push him in it". I may add, his own vocabulary was not quite so delicate as my interpretation. I thought the suggestions were excrutiatingly funny.

For the first time we inherited an old grease eroded gas stove left by the previous tenants. This was conveniently placed by the coal cupboard door, near enough to cause the coalman to curse horribly when shooting his two hundred weight sack, with difficulty. Projecting from the wall was a gas jet which burned with an open flame dimly illuminating the surroundings with a flickering glow, which on many occasions was turned low for economy.

Mother was essentially a saver as father was not. So many times this jet was blown out by draught leaving the gas to merrily escape to the danger of us all. Still, no attempt was made to purchase the fittings to enable a mantled globe to be installed. That would be a waste of money!

No locks functioned, no bolts were fitted to the back door. "That was the landlords job". The outside lavatory door was skilfully fitted with a length of string by father. This enabled the occupier to hold the door shut, and keep the intruders at bay, and so not disturb whoever may be in deep concentration, while in the position of that famous piece of sculpture "The Thinker". At regular intervals this convenience was blocked by portions of *The News of the World*, which were cut up by myself and hung on a nail for hygiene purposes, after it had served its initial purpose as a newspaper. It will therefore be observed it retained its content to its final destruction.

Washing day! – this stands out as one of the most dreadful days of the week. It usually started very early on Monday. The worst part being that sections of the wash littered the house until Thursday. Mothers organising ability was not all that good. Monday morning saw me at my first job of bringing in the washing stool from underneath the outside shelter. This was a ramshackle affair built and designed by dear father who, like myself, was the world's worst carpenter.

It was precariously lodged against the dividing fence of the terraced houses. The fence also being in a poor state of repair and apparently owned by no-one in particular, as each landlord refused to acknowledge it as his responsibility.

With the stool in the scullery (better known as the "wash house") the next ritual was to foster up any burnable rubbish, such as old lino, scraps of wood, cardboard and even my "Penny Dreadfuls" if I had not the foresight to hide them beforehand. Mother then proceeded to light the copper. To use coal in

Rear soldier, driver G. J. Walker, Salisbury Plain 1915.

this cauldron was considered far too extravagant, even though the fire usually went out several times through lack of fuel. However, a boil up was necessary, not only for cleanliness, but as a show of prestige to the neighbours, with all casting critical eyes on each other's personal belongings. Billowing from the clothes line, that ran the length of the garden, the spotless results of mothers scrubbing, denied adverse criticism.

After a hasty breakfast, I made off to school with all speed to escape "the late line", which meant embarrassment, black mark and inevitably the cane, colloquially known as "the big stick". On returning home from school at noon I was greeted with the clouds of steam rising from the copper which contained a bubbling mass of grey water in which swirled, among other things, father's long pants and socks. Mother, with her redoubtable copper stick for stirring, which was frayed through constant immersion in boiling water, and at intervals for throwing at marauding cats, thankfully removed her coarse apron, for a deserved respite.

Cold meat from Sunday joint, bread and home made pickles was all that was expected on this day for lunch. This had its bright side as by its simplicity was served in time for me to return to school in good time, without the breathless rush to escape the ever ominous late line.

On returning home from afternoon school, I still saw mother in her bustling manner finishing off and cleaning the scullery of its chaotic condition and collecting in the hoards of washing, if dry. The smell of "Sunlight Soap" and the view of fluttering intimate clothing, is a scene to remain in my memory. So, too, is the melodious tones of mother singing – probably with relief, that the end had come to a hard industrious day. Only to be followed on the next by intermittent ironing, folding, etc. These were far more pleasant days, combining the warmth of the open kitchen stove with sundry irons heating on its hob. The fascination of observing the method of testing the heat by lightly spitting on them or dangerously holding them near a cheek or, more foolishly still, wetting a finger and actually touching the heated surface.

Mother's repertoire was varied and many of the ballads were sad and sentimental. "The hymns my mother used to sing", was one which took in a complete batch of hymns. While some of the songs are still known to-day, I submit just a few. This one in particular was rendered with true feminine venom. My vivid imagination played havoc while I envisaged the scene of tragedy:

Men were deceivers ever,
I've often heard folks say
But believe me when I tell you this

You'll want me back some day!

(This was also vociferously sung by cousin Ivy Burt, who had a strong nasal cockney voice, deplored in those days, but strangely popular today, by the so-called vocalists of various groups.

Then there was a sadly mournful one:

To lose or to part
Would break my old heart
The dear faded leaf of a rose
And oh how she sighed and bitterly cried
How we miss her, well 'Gawd' only knows,
We were happy as children in childhood
As the ways of her heart clearly shows,
To lose or to part would break my old heart
That dear faded leaf of a rose!

And more sadness:

Are we to part like this Bill?
Are we to part this way?
Is it to be, you or me,
Don't be a frightened to say,
Is it all over between us?
Are we to say goodbye –
Friends we'll be – you and me
For the sake of the days gone by!

Here comes the reconciliation:

For old times sake
Let us forget and forgive,
For old times sake
Don't let your enmity live
Life's too short to quarrel
Hearts are too precious to break,
Shake hands and let us be friends
For old times sake.

Of course, father had to apply his version and, when singing in his strangled voice, he substituted the last line with "shake hands and let us be friends for Jesus Christ's sake". This brought the inevitable reproach from mother, "Now, George, stop it, you'll be paid out, you mark my words". Mother strongly believed in the vengeance of Christ.

One song that always struck me at the time as so emotional that I envisaged a faithful son, swearing his love to his grey haired dear old mother with his hand on his heart and tears in his eyes, viz:

Mother, I love you,
What more can a loving son do,
Don't let your tears run down your cheek
I'll bring my wages to you every week,
I'll always stand by you.
What more can a loving son do.
You've worked for me a long, long time,
And now I must work for you.

How about that for a loving son? Of course he would most certainly have to secure employment first! It was no effort for me to see that strapping lad with blue eyes and curly blonde hair facing the world in defence of his grey haired old mother. I presume his father was either dead or his son did not care how he fared, a real mum's boy!

"Till the sands of the desert run cold" is probably a better known ballad and when this was sung at our war time sing songs, (another lost pleasure) tears were copiously shed by mother who usually retired to the kitchen, while the song was rendered by sister Winnie. She was the possessor of a stentorian soprano voice, backed up by Albert, her young man at the piano, (He jilted her later, and we all considered it a lucky escape for him).

The reason for mother's tears was that brother George was posted to Mesopotamia during the 1914-18 war and the desert was, of course, synonymous with his absence.

His farewell party, as all were, had a strangely false atmosphere. While all joined in the laughter, jokes and songs, no-one envisaged the persons to whom this party had been arranged, may not return.

Our whole family went to Victoria Station to bid their final farewell. It may be hard to imagine whole train-loads of soldiers, with full equipment, including rifles in hand and bayonets sheathed on their belts, steel helmets and kit bags, in organised chaos.

All were crowded in compartments, some on the platform pacifying their crying families, others looking lost and completely alone.

It happened to be my first experience on the underground railway. Lifts were mainly the means of descent, and each train coach was controlled by a guard, who operated the open air iron latticed gates. He would stand opposite the entrance and, with a nasal shout "mind the gates", would operate a lever causing the gates to close in a concertina fashion, accompanied by a resounding clash. The seats were of an interwoven straw material, quite strong and like the seats of St. Bartholomew's Hospital, extremely shiny from use. My interest in this new kind of travel intrigued me more than the khaki clad victims, whose lease of life was in the balance. At the age of ten, the full meaning of war was not apparent.

Nevertheless, the parties during that war, in spite of the awful casualties, shortage of goods and food, were many. Almost every family was either welcoming home a service man, or bidding him farewell and so making an escape from horror and terror that that awful holocaust was causing.

A non treating law was passed to curtail the drinking of government beer. This weakened version of the peace time variety, was much in evidence to drown your sorrows. Food was scarce unless you could penetrate the black market. In 1917 the U Boat menace was at its peak. Rumours, true or otherwise, were that stocks of the country's food were almost exhausted. Stallholders even imposed a form of rationing. Two pounds of potatoes only for each person. I was once beckoned by a housewife, who thrust a bag in one hand, and money in the other. She then entreated me to obtain two pounds of spuds. For services rendered I received a penny. This instance led me to the queues on Saturdays soliciting my services, and earning extra pocket money.

Mother would never queue for potatoes, she used swedes or pease pudding as a substitute. Often Sunday dinner consisted of a herring each, with bread of a dirty grey colour know as "Standard Bread".

Matters were far more serious than realised! Naturally, the first world war period made a great impression on me at the time, and still holds a fascinating interest of the history leading up to it. The night in which the first Zeppelin was brought down at Cuffley by Lt. Robinson V.C. was one which will always remain vivid in my memory. The acclamation of the people and the excitement that, at last we had hit back having been so impotent against this invasion of Germanic horror.

Father, in his usual but foolish manner, was standing in the garden ignoring the falling shrapnel from our shells, which were unable to reach the height of the Zepps, came bounding in the kitchen. The rest of the family sat, in the true British fashion, sustaining their fortitude by drinking tea! Not, I may add, with aplomb, but as usual when raids were in progress, tea was one of the first thoughts, and gave a reassurance. Father's entry with an exclamation "we've got the bastard!" brought us all to our feet, with a concerted rush to the front door. An amazing sight met our eyes, in the form of a flaming Zepp which seemed to descend so slowly lighting the sky, accompanied by a roar on par with a cup final, mixed with clapping. En-mass hysteria in its entirety! This can be well understood, as it was our first, but not the last, of that long looked for revenge.

Our particular family ran with the rest of the occupants of our small street to the end of it, in order to see the final flaming descent, of the hated enemy aircraft.

We were situated on a slight hill giving us an unobstructed view. Having been always risk conscious, I returned to collect mother's black Gladstone bag containing cash and heirlooms, plus the proof of the families legitimacy, and a collection of twopenny Prudential policies. These were always on hand – in the event of an emergency. The valuable bag had been left behind to the wide open world. With excitement at its highest, I mingled with the crowd, in a vain attempt to locate the family as the emotion gradually subsided, and people who before had not even known each other, had exhausted themselves in animated discussion, and a sporadic trek, was made to their respective homes. Father had revelled in recounting his eye witness account of observing the Zeppelin, in the search lights, prior to the brave pilot bringing it down. The family eventually returned home to find the front door wide open and the famous treasure bag left on the kitchen table, gone! Cries of despair accompanied by hot and cold sweats, finally it was decided to seek a policeman. They always brought a feeling of security and assistance even if they did not bring the bag. The consternation turned to relief, when I returned some time later with the famous bag intact.

I had exploited every minute of being out in the early hours of the morning, chatting to my street friends, whilst wallowing in the excitement. I still had possession of the black bag, and the risk of mother having apoplexy finally disappeared.

The sight presented by the first daylight raid was a paramount example of incredible effrontery. It was Saturday morning 13th June 1917, a large squadron of Gothas flying in perfect formation over London on that sunny Saturday morning. We were witnessing the explosive puffs of shells breaking harmlessly below them. They were passing over to central London with complete indifference. It was as exciting to me as it was frustrating to our ack ack batteries.

Mother sitting on the stairs which faced the open front door, tearfully entreating me to "come in" whilst I stood enthralled at the first actual sight of the enemy committing this initial barbarous act.

It was pathetic to see people more stunned than frightened. The sheer surprise of this completely unexpected act of hostility on helpless civilians, could hardly be believed. Remember that when someone remarks that we perpetrated the same act, remind them it was quite a time before the English retaliated, following the cry from the press and general public for "reprisals".

Secretly, I used to enjoy the raids, not realising the horror of the ultimate result, or witnessing the actual fatalities. In latter years, whilst serving in the National Fire Service during the second world war, I found it less enjoyable, especially when confronting the casualties. All that concerned me then was I could be up late at night, and have cups of tea with the family at all hours of the night and probably be late for school without getting the cane, or even miss it completely.

There was a period when the raids were intensified with considerable regularity for two weeks. This may appear trivial when comparing the long periods of day and night bombardment in the Second World War, but remember here was something never before experienced and most alarming.

It caused many to make for the first individual evacuations from London, not an organised performance as experienced in latter years.

I must reiterate by emphasising this was the first time ever that explosives rained down on a virtually unprotected civilian population and whatever history may be written in the future it was the Hun and no other nation who first started this type of warfare. Similarly they initiated submarine attacks on merchant ships, perpetrated poison gas and flame throwers – all used with complete indifference. In the second war when they were on the receiving end, whining protests were made against our retaliation. After the disclosure of the concentration camps with their attendant horrors, I can only confirm the ancient biblical writing "an eye for an eye".

It is most peculiar that such a brilliant nation should retain that strain of cruelty and arrogance for centuries. It was in this present century that retribution came. Pointless as war is, survival is paramount. I shudder to imagine our lot had Hitler been the victor. We should all be unstinting in our praise for all who played their part, and to our leader Winston Churchill, who had the full measure of that gang of thugs.

Returning to the intensive raid period my mother decided to accompany me to Sawbridgeworth, and stay at step grandmother's and so escape the terrifying nights which were so consistent. We left father, Arch, and three sisters to fend for themselves (Hilda was now a Red Cross nurse and George was on active service). Sawbridgeworth was only about 25 or 30 miles away yet it offered a haven from the bombs, but not the barrage. On our arrival we were greeted by a forthright remark from the formidable step mother of my parent, "It's no use you coming here! It's just as bad as up there" pointing skywards. The welcome was not that effusive.

Apparently granny's concern was the barrage being quite prodigious. The ack-ack guns were ringed around London quite a number being in Sawbridgeworth. On that night they began their evening chorus, creating more noise than experienced in London but without the dull crump of bombs. These were quite noticeable by their absence while we were preparing to retire. Step Granny's reaction at the beginning of a raid was quite opposite to ours, she just blew out the one and only candle, and jumped into bed leaving us nonplussed to grope about in the dark.

Our usual reaction was to get up and light up and make the tea! On reflection, it was country logic perhaps, and was rather more sensible to act in such a way, although they had not witnessed or experienced a bomb episode.

The following day saw the arrival of the three sisters seeking succour. The popularity they received from the troops on the guns during their brief stay was obvious in a very short time.

They apparently soon put aside the terrors of war, to the joys of fraternising with the troops. I can only assume this by the showers of apples, walnuts and all kinds of produce that were scarce to the civilian population, being endowed by the soldiers, billetted in and around.

I was young and innocent and obviously cannot elaborate on their escapades, which is rather a pity. It may have made this story a bestseller, who knows? However, after a while everyone got used to war and its contributory factors. As no official evacuation scheme or monetary benefits were in being after a while, it had to be accepted and to return home and "carry on as usual".

Sister Ada, the eldest, was the most excitable and impressionable of all and offered up the most marvellous "off the cuff" prayers to the Almighty during the raids which even embarrassed me as a child. Years later, during the second world war, she was buried in the cellar of her own house as a result of a rocket bomb while all other occupants were killed. A successful rescue was carried out, aided by her using a whistle kept on a necklace for that purpose. The sound so directed the civil defence to the spot where she was imprisoned, in terrifying circumstances. It does appear her faith in prayer had not been in vain.

Although we were near the bombing targets, we sustained one broken scullery window. This was caused by a nose cap of our own shells, bouncing off next door's roof making a resounding crash. This event accentuated Ada's forceful prayers, requesting the Lord "if we are to go – please take us now". I was always in a confused mind on these occasions.

In contrast to the air raid events, we had the visitation of a burglar who had no difficulty in opening our boltless back door. His tinkering with the gas meter, which was devoid of cash being a quarterly account one, awakened mother, who promptly awoke father. By the time father had found his boots under the bed, secured his trousers safely – procured the heavy mahogany curtain pole for defence, and clumped down the stairs, the miscreant had fled, with time to spare.

I was awakened by a terrific crash! Caused by a shoulder charge by father, who found the kitchen door secured by a chair placed under the handle. Without thought, I leaped from bed and ran downstairs, to find father swinging the pole around in the darkness and uttering dire threats to no one in particular. With trembling hands he then lit the gas and contemplated a scene of destruction. There had been a spate of petty thefts in rows of houses, so mother with remarkable presence of mind, opened the bedroom window screaming, "Burglars! Help! Police!" This hysterical cry caused the appearance of a further villain. He had calmly opened the front door of the next house and ran down the street. A further shout from mother of "There he goes George" electrified father into instant action. He was slightly encumbered by his pole and also his trailing boots laces. Needless to say, the miscreant escaped leaving a street aroused, as much, as if there had been an air raid. We still did not have a bolt fixed, not while there was a chair to lodge under the door handle. As an added precaution I placed tin cans at the rear, thus creating our own patent burglar alarm.

The event made quite a diversion from the air raids, and was a source of discussion for weeks. This type of petty crime was so rare, compared with today's criminality.

Mother and father remained in these premises long after I had ventured into lodgings, which is another story. Briefly, sister May had married a cousin, who was a dour and shrewd, if not a mean person. He, who we will call Dick bought 14, Byfield Road for the exorbitant amount of £200 as an occupied premises. He then moved in with his family of one baby girl, graciously allowing my parents to remain. It was 1929, I was twenty-three years of age. I could foresee friction, so I sought pastures new, which brought problems new.

The dog that ran sideways when drunk, also aunt Ada's pets.

CHAPTER 4

The First Wedding held at 14 Byfield

THE initial wedding in the Walker family between Ada the eldest and Fred Alsopp was of such importance that the war was even forgotten. It was early in 1915, the weather was beautiful when the day of days dawned.

Excitement had been building up for months, mother's shillings had been deposited each week at 'Garnhams' (High Street Glass and China Emporium). The object in view was a 'nice cut glass vase' or 'tea service' for the wedding present.

Arguments regarding bridesmaids and what dresses or colours to wear etc, were evident, and causing scandalous gossip, interspersed with vociferous differences of opinion.

The barrel of beer was ordered, and set up, in father's tool shed attached to the rear of the house. This was his natural and only contribution he could successfully organise – and sample!

On entering the kitchen that morning, from the bedroom I witnessed a hive of activity in the laying of the wedding breakfast, in an already electric atmosphere. As far as my breakfast was concerned I was hurriedly dispatched with a slice of bread and jam and firmly instructed to sit by sister Winnie's sewing machine, conveniently housed in the corner. Furthermore, in loud and strident tones, I was told to "Keep out of the way" and "We don't want any trouble from you today!"

Being quite used to such remarks did not deter my inner excitement, accentuated by the anticipation of sampling the jellies and custard, already on view.

In due course the relations and guests arrived. The first of these was 'fat' Aunt Ada and Uncle Bill. The former was mother's youngest sister and my favourite aunt, who was as jolly as she was stout, and possessed two striking minor disabilities. One of these was a rigid middle finger, which was most apparent when that lady was holding a glass of beer, to which she was most partial. Secondly, her right eye was rather smaller than its opposite number. So, when sampling a new brew of that liquid, her eye screwed up to smaller proportions, while the offending finger would be pointing accusingly to whoever she was addressing. Her invariable remark to mother would be "terrible stuff Poll like poison" but, poison or not, she always managed to drink the remainder.

Uncle Bill was rather short and sartorily elegant, hair smartly parted in the middle with each side ending in a slight curl, a well waxed spiky moustache, adorning a rubicond complexion composed of a series of red vein-like lines, very typical of a music hall chairman. His vocation had a bearing on his florid appearance. He held a responsible position in 'Savilles Brewery' (now defunct) at Stratford East.

He possessed a likeable dog that always accompanied its master to work, and often returned quite inebriated, which could be detected when the animal ran home 'side-ways'. (See Photo)

A pin of beer was delivered at regular intervals to their flat and kept under the stairs which obviously assisted in perpetuating the complexion of both. In spite of this, I never saw either the worse for drink or miserable.

The day was sunny, bright and warm, which enabled the garden – such as it was – to make room for the reception overflow. Apropos to the good weather no fire was needed in the 'Parlour'. This also was a godsend, as it usually billowed with smoke whenever this rare occasion occurred. Mother always promised the flue would be swept, but it never materialised the chimney often caught light which saved the expense. Ada, the blushing bride, an exceedingly excitable female, was strangely subdued but nevertheless happy, it was her great day. Fred Alsopp, the opposite number to be joined in holy wedlock, was a tall gentleman in the real sense, with rather a Sherlock Holmes type of face with the exception of rather thick lips, but apart from this he was a strong character type and marked with intelligence. Proof of this was when he volunteered for the Navy and became A First Class Signaller and finally Lieutenant, after completing active service on various ships.

Prior to this I had been decked out in a new suit with continued admonishings 'to behave myself' 'keep the suit clean', etc. and had been occupied for what seemed an age, looking out for the rare sight of an automobile to stop outside our house.

My frenzied announcement to this fact resulted in hurried arrangements for those departing in style. The beleagured taxi driver making endless journeys to St Saviour's Church, Markhouse Road a high church boasting of a school, also a convent-cum-medical clinic. This was a boon to the many poor and the physical needs it provided were better understood than the spiritual ones.

At last it was our turn to be conveyed in the one and only taxi. I accompanied mother, fat Aunt Ada, and many more. We were rather crowded, which left Aunt Ada quite close to the door on the little collapsible seat.

Bride and Groom – Fred and Ada.

The driver in his hurry to get away accelerated when emerging from Byfield Road and while swinging round to the right, nearly deposited Aunt Ada in the middle of Queen's Road. The off-side door had blown open, and but for the heroic action and quick thought of Uncle Bill, although he had had a good top up of Mann & Crossmans XXXX (Double XX), as he professionally called it, he managed to grab auntie. Mind you there was plenty to grab, and he thankfully succeeded in bringing her back to the already well populated taxi.

Meanwhile the driver ploughed on regardless, and quite oblivious of the near catastrophe that might have turned the wedding into an ultimate funeral. However, we arrived at St. Saviour's, hats askew and in exuberant spirits.

Of the ceremony, I have but vague recollections, it was the celebrations that stand out. I was guilty of sneaking to my mother by informing her that brother Arch age 15 and cousin Will Lambert were smoking on their walk back from church. Many who rode to church preferred to walk back, possibly because of the 'Common Gate' or the 'Markhouse Arms'. The last mentioned was popularly known as 'Bert Crows' was a magnet to those who intended to make it a momentous day.

During the early evening, the urchins in the street took great fun in standing on our front wall on which were mounted the usual decorative iron railings, and peeping at the festivities. Some of the guests were endeavouring to dance on virtually a 'postage stamp' floor, to the strains of our German piano, ably mastered by Albert Ellingham. His parents owned the baker's shop in Markhouse Road, which resulted in a wedding cake at a wholesale price.

It was inevitable father had to get drunk! But only slightly so. I positively remember his voice that always boomed when he was tipsy. The tone rose at the end of a sentence. He tipped the barrel of beer to obtain the final drops, including the residue, remarking "there's life in the old dog yet!"

However, before the evening drew to a close he was persuaded to sing his usual party song. Inevitably with feigned reluctance and a strangled voice in keeping with a monotonous tune he burst forth as follows:

MICKY DUNNS PARTY

Last night I was invited by a pal named Micky Dunn
To a party he was giving where we'd bound to have some fun,
Meself and Dan MacGinnish, we were dressed in all our best
So we thought we'd look quite as flash as all the rest.
The clock was striking seven we were ready for to start,
We drove to the party in O'Grady's donkey cart.

The guests were all assembled we all sat down to dine,
There was everything from pigs cheek to elderberry wine,

Chorus
First we had some cabbage and some home cured ham,
Eggs fried with treacle stuff and bread and fat and jam,
Herrings stewed with pastry, taters on the boil,
And the gravy it was flavoured with railway wagon oil,
Egg soup, camels hump, and other kinds of fish,
Mushrooms and rhubarb floating round the dish,
Highly flavoured sucking pigs toasted nice and brown,
But the beer was struck with thunder so we couldn't wash it down.
The eating it was over and the pipers they did bring
Every man and woman in the house they had to sing,
It was Mary Ann Matilda who got up to sing the first
And before her song was finished her windpipe she did burst,
The next one to sing was Mary Ann O'Bride,
She rattled off 'The Battle of the Bile'
Fagan said she couldn't sing, he was called a liar
Mary collared hold of him and slung him on the fire,
Limpy Bobby Brallinghan got up to take his part,
The house was in an uproar and ructions soon did start,
Long Mac the navvy in the middle of the floor
Laid hold of Barney, and flung him out the door,
A copper appeared upon the scene
He looked as green as grass, Barney collared hold of him
And flung him on his arse* trousers,
He blew his whistle up came a score or more
It ended in an uproar and finished in a fight
Which busted up the party at Mick Dunns last night.

*When this word was used mother's reply would inevitably be "Now George, that's enough".

We had endured this rendering over the years.

The happy couple departed after the festive board had been completed and the bride had changed into the appropriate travelling clothing i.e. navy blue costume bedecked in braid and high neck lace blouse, belted waist and a monstrous hat of the period.

Ada's previous employer arrived in a spanking horse and trap to convey the exuberant couple to St. James Street station en-route to a venue, which to me was shrouded in mystery: 'Felixstowe'!

The only seaside resort I was aware of was 'Southend'. Wherever this latest obscure place was I was unaware, but it sounded wonderful. Farewells were made accompanied by previously concealed confetti, and we were left to continue the celebration. Although the central attraction had gone the party spirit remained. This resulted in the whole company solemnly toasting the departed couple at frequent intervals.

On their return dear Ada and Fred took up residence in 34, Chatham Road, E.17 a modest terraced house in a genteel road. Fred became a sailor boy very soon and whenever possible Ada followed him to various ports, wherever his ship was based. Sometimes in Wales and even Ireland.

And so ended a great event as far as the Walker clan were concerned.

After the vicitudes of war, Fred, my hero, tragically fell a victim of the flu epidemic which swept through the country as an aftermath of that terrible conflict. So poor Fred's life, after being spared so many times, was terminated by a minute germ, that defied all the medical skills and was reminiscent of 'The Great Plague', *The Spanish Flu.**

He passed away shortly after the Armistice. Funerals were being conducted with monotonous regularity each day.

---

*The Spanish Flu originated quite suddenly in Spain in 1918 and very soon became a pandemic and was termed "The Spanish Lady" over one billion in the world were affected. I too experienced its effect, which left one weak and vulnerable.

In the U.K. approximately 23,000 died. In some cases persons dropped dead in the street, without warning. Capt. Leefe Robinson V.C. the first pilot to bring down a raiding Zepelin, was a victim, as also another famous airman, Alan McLeod. After an exceptional war record, including combat against "Richthofens Flying Circus", he succumed, on his home-coming to Canada. Although vaccination now, could be made, it has strangely been consistently ignored. The Plague faded and disappeared as quickly as it began, having been at its height for 120 days. There are many variations of the virus, and new strains appear intermittently. It is believed to be dormant in pigs and horses, and it is possible to re-occur.

CHAPTER 5

School Days

THE most impressionable days in one's life are undoubtedly those of the school period. They stand out forcibly, some in fear and others in sheer joy.

Mornings always began with a cacophony of factory hooters of various tones, at equal interludes. Mother professed to be conversant with the exact times they registered. "That's the five to eight or the ten to nine etc." she would observe, in a most pedantic manner. I can only conclude the factories had their own particular reasons, regarding this long period of early morning chorus. At the cessation of hooters came the clang of school bells. There were four schools within hearing, each supplying its melodious chimes. They were Queens Road, Markhouse Road, St Saviours, and last, and not the least important, my own venerable seat of learning Gamuel Road. This contributed a beautiful flat cracked sound, rung with monotonous regularity by the favourite boy. He was nominated for the task by his general behaviour and early habits. He was expected to be at school, well in advance of the sloths, who were perpetually late.

Looking ahead to 1947 I was unfortunately diagnosed as a peptic ulcer sufferer which resulted in changing my life style completely. The reason for mentioning this fact is I am partly convinced that this ailment initiated from my school days, coupled with mother's heavy but, worst of all, late meals.

For example, dinner time during school 12-2, dinner period now of course referred to as lunch, was always prepared about ten minutes before returning to school.

This meant a hurried wolfing of whatever it may be, followed immediately by desperately running to school, with a distended stomach, and a palpitating heart. The latter accentuated by being in fear of getting into the 'late line' and the subsequent cane.

If this misdemeanour occurred twice in a given period a black mark was entered against you which affected "your character". This ominous and mysterious sealed document was handed to pupils on leaving school, strictly to be opened only by either parent. It was considered of paramount importance, and referred to in hushed tones by the recipients.

My first job when arriving home at mid-day, was to fetch mother's beer in a bottle from an off licence quite half a mile away. She was partial to a certain brew as opposed to a contemporary one, which could have been purchased only a few yards distant from our house.

It was amusing to me even at that age, that the law did not allow a child to buy beer in a jug until the age of 14. I was extremely proud when I achieved that maturity to be able to perform this act, by taking a jug and feeling very grown up. However, the law in its great wisdom allowed a child to obtain intoxicating liquor in a bottle providing it was sealed by the off licence owner.

This he or she did by wetting a gum backed piece of paper in the spilt beer on the counter which was always in evidence, and slapping it over the cork and on to the bottle, which immediately fell off as it was handed over.

I presume the object of this was to deter the child from taking a swig at the flat, smelly stuff that to me was most revolting. This revulsion, of course, changed later in life. This brilliant piece of legislation like many, was futile in its careless application.

I shall never forget that heavy quart bottle surreptitiously "hidden" in a string bag, that closed up at the neck, leaving the contents quite visible. On one fatal occasion mother must have been extra thirsty, as at 1.45 I was told to get a further pint of ale having already made the purchase as soon as I had arrived home from school. Bearing in mind it was time for me to return to school I pleaded the fact that I would be late. It was to no avail!

So once again the quart bottle was relentlessly placed in the string bag! One may enquire why a quart bottle? Well, there was always the chance of getting a little over a pint in a quart bottle, whereas by offering a pint one, it would defeat that little drop from the extra pull which the pump operator invariably gave, known as a little 'make weight'.

This custom of "make weight" was not only confined to beer, it also occurred when purchasing bread, ice cream, or other commodities. 'The little extra' habit was common place i.e. the loaf was weighed and if below 2 lbs a piece was cut to 'make up the official weight'.

The term "make weight" was common place, to various commodities. Another case, when purchasing ice cream in a glass cone, from an ice cream barrow, the purchaser would consume the cream, hand the cone back, and ask "for a taster Jack"! sometimes resulting in a dab of "ice", the cheaper variety, previously mentioned.

The little squirt of beer, was a regular custom. These quaint habits have, among many, gone for ever!

Incidentally the glass cones used by the Italian Ice Cream vendor were for persons who stood by the barrow. They consumed the cream and thoroughly cleaned the glass with their tongue. When finished 'Jack' plunged the glass shaped cornet into a well used bucket of water, and returned the receptacle for the next customer, thus passing on the flow of bacteria ad-infinitum.

Gamuel Road Infant School 1910 Christmas play – Stars and Moonbeams. Second from right front row the author. Top back row 1st right Willie Webber.

Much the same happened with beer glasses, although the beer drinkers did not make a habit of licking round the glass.

A tearful very resentful child went on that second errand. On returning from the off licence with the bottle duly charged and the seal, legally and dutifully applied, I began to swing the hated bag in a temper, coupled with malice and frustration.

Whilst in this resentful mood, calamity occurred! It collided with some iron railings which proved to be a tougher material than the contents of the bag. The string bag was so much lighter, but my heart considerably heavier. My fear was indescribable, and the whacking best forgotten. I was experiencing the interpretation of the aforementioned "Bossicks". In spite of it all, I felt a wonderful sense of satisfaction, and considered it was well worth it.

One must not get too bad an impression of mother. She was not meaningly cruel and never realised the mental torture and abhorrence I had of having to perform repetitive errands. Being made to return to the place from which I had just left was one of her most irritating habits. In much later life this forgetfulness was inflicted on poor father, who became my substitute for errand services.

Apart from Gamuel Road School:

There was an interuption in 1917-1918 when I attended a church school at Wareside, a village in Hertfordshire, in which I underwent a traumatic experience which may be described in the future. However, the staff at Gamuel Road would put many of the teachers today to shame. Their dedication and teaching ability produced a large percentage of pupils with a degree of education far higher than any similar school of today. Above all they commanded and obtained the respect and obedience of 95% of the pupils. The other 5% were mainly poor whose home life was rough and bordering on to a criminal element. They were more to be pitied than condemned.

The Herring family were a typical example and unfortunately were abysmally poor and suffering from malnutrition, with parents of low mentality. 'Bony Herring', one of the tribe, was at school at the same period as myself was aptly named. The nickname needs no explanation. He made history in fighting with a teacher, by attacking him with a map pole, this being a large pole with an S shaped hook at the top used for carrying a wall map to whatever position it was required, and other duties including opening and shutting the long sliding windows. He completed his studies in an approved school or sometimes known as the 'Truant' school, a kind of schoolboys glass house. Nowadays he would probably have been benignly reprimanded by a social worker, whilst the teacher would be up before the education board and told to be more tolerant. To prove the worth of the discipline metered out, poor old Boney made good and was a credit when he left.

The Herring family, I cannot remember how many. They were produced with monotonous regularity and were all extremely agile. In fact, the family would have made an exceptional acrobatic act. They all performed the most dangerous and outrageous '**Dags**', the term used for tricks. They were as much at home walking on their hands as their feet. They caused great merriment to all the class, by walking round the classroom and between the gangways in the alternative position, when the teacher was absent. If caught in the act they were rewarded by a taste of the cane, which in no way deterred them, and was taken with the stoicism of a Red Indian. Cartwheels were included in the performance, and double somersaults, off an extremely high wooden partition that stood in isolation outside the open air toilets were a daily practice. The main purpose of this partition was to exclude the ablutions from public gaze, regardless of the fact that the W.C.s were open to all and sundry.

Before mentioning one of their most notorious escapades, I must introduce the staff, to whom I had great respect, beginning with the Head "Old 'Witty'" or Mr. Withycombe. A fine leader with iron grey wavy hair, with a matching moustache. A strong intelligent face, stern grey eyes, which at times twinkled, and were enhanced by crinkles at the side of each. I can only remember him wearing a light grey, lord of the manor suit. He was a man who stood no nonsense and a firm favourite with us all. He also possessed a grand sense of humour. In fact, when any teacher was absent we welcomed him as a substitute. He would usually give us a task to write a story and then depart for the rest of the morning. During the afternoon we were allowed to read out aloud our efforts, to the amusement of both he and ourselves, with his critical comments, combined with corrections. This freedom of expression proved most instructive and entertaining.

Next, Mr Ridler, nom de plume, just 'old Ridler' of the 7th standard, a martinet feared by most, a mighty wielder of the cane, known as 'the stick'. As a final finisher to the leavers he was an excellent, but heartless man, sometimes cruel. A short dapper balding person whose wisps of hair, failed in the endeavour to conceal his pate. Gold rimmed spectacles, a well waxed spike moustache, revealing thin sarcastic lips. A gold watch and chain adorned his dove grey vest. The timepiece was constantly consulted, with raised eyebrows over watery pale eyes. His silk handkerchief equally in use polishing his glasses. Invariably garbed in a brown suit, and a high stiff collar, his fire cracked ox blood shoes, shone "like a sovereign up a sweeps arse" as my father was apt to remark. There is the picture of "Ridler"! By present day standards, he would probably be termed as a near sadist, particularly for his sheer delight in corporal punishment. For example, he would leave the classroom, then quickly retrace his steps very quietly to peer over the baize (which covered half of the glass panes in the classroom doors) in order to select his victims. Being of short stature, we often could see his balding pate, prior to raising himself on tip-toe to achieve this effort.

More often than not, the din that exploded, after he had left the room, would have muffled any returning steps.

Having once been caught in this revelry and burst of pent up freedom, I always kept a sharp look-out for his shiny head that came into view before his gimlet eyes appeared. A quick call of "cave"! or just "Ridler"! was all that was necessary, to foil his anticipated pleasure of wielding his beloved ash plant. This loving instrument was surreptiously kept under the side flap of his desk*.

His specialised subjects were maths and Shakespeare. The latter I revelled in. Even to-day I enjoy quoting the famous speeches of Mark Anthony and Brutus, plus acting Shylock.

The former orations had to be delivered over a 'T' square, covered with a duster representing a dead Caesar in the front of the class. When it came to 'there lies the body of Caesar" it took all my willpower to refrain from laughing, which had happened on earlier occasions – with dire results.

His obsession for maths went too far. On Friday afternoons, when all other classes were enjoying readings from Dickens, Stephenson, Ballentyne and the like, dear Ridler would trot out "the Tontine" to polish up our mental arithmetic. This resulted in terrific eyestrain, plus the possible tickle from the cane. *Note* for those not familiar with the Tontine, this roll of white linen substance on which a mass of figures were printed (some in £.s.d.) was enclosed in a case with roller at the top and bottom. By exposing several lines of figures, we were instructed to add up by vision and pass oral answers. By the turn of one roller the sum could be changed for a second test and so on. This "relaxing" pastime, often caused watery eyes in endeavouring to complete this onerous task. There were a very few who appeared to enjoy this

---

*Teachers were not supposed to own their own cane. The correct procedure was to send a boy for the school cane (the big stick) and the black book kept under the supervision of the Headmaster. This was a formidable heavy cane, greatly feared and, even worse, was to have ones name entered in the black book. Although we were aware of this ruling we preferred the stinging cut of Ridler's smaller cane than the dull heavy throb caused by the permitted partly blackened legal instrument of punishment, lodged with the headmaster.

Mr. Wood, the expert rubber thrower, with myself directly in front of him. Headmaster on left.

pastime. Some made the pretence of enjoying this task, solely to curry favour, much to the disgust of many.

Standard 6 was commanded by Mr. Newton – affectionately known as 'old Newt'. He was the most popular teacher of the whole bunch and the absolute opposite to Ridler. A very tall craggy man, an excellent teacher who taught without putting fear into the pupils, he dressed and looked more like a country gentleman farmer, always garbed in a loose fitting heavy cloth grey suit, trousers extremely baggy. Sartorial elegance was sadly lacking. In fact he was a keen gardener which probably assisted in his untidy appearance. He often briefed his favourite pupils to bring in bags of leaf mould from the nearby Epping Forest. We all vied for this task, unaware of being lawbreakers. He encouraged dramatics and comedy, producing a nigger minstrel troupe. I was delighted in being "corner-man" asking the chairman various questions, e.g. "can youse tell me masser interlocutor, why an egg am like the Union Jack", "no sah why" etc. – "Cos no powah on earth can pull it down", shrieks of laughter. I have always enjoyed histrionics, in fact the whole family were all inclined towards entertaining. In the case of sister Winnie, myself and brothers Arch and Geo, we all had a brief spell of semi-professional performing. It was old Newt who asked our parents if Arch and I could take up dramatic art. This meant cash, a commodity that was needed for more important purposes so our parents observed. The suggestion fell on stony ground.

Among old Newtons hobbies was motor cycling and we all stood in awe when he arrived on his belt driven Triumph 500cc motor cycle, a rare sight in those days. After I left school, Newton was appointed headmaster to a grammar school and sadly met an early and untimely death as a result of a motor car accident. A tragic ending to a perfect English Gentleman.

After leaving school, I often visited Newton who on one confidential occasion remarked in a most philosophical manner, 'Mr Ridler reminds me of a little boy who once found a penny in the gutter, and from that day on he constantly looked in the gutter. He forgot there was a sky and sun above and a host of beautiful things! Ridler taught me Shakespeare – Newton taught me philosophy.

Fifth standard saw Mr Wood or "Woody", another likeable tall man with a spiky black moustache. Although he had not the personality of Newton he was nevertheless a good sort – encouraged sport, taught well and had a marvellous marksmanship in throwing a rubber at any boy who was not attending, or dosing off. He possessed remarkable accuracy with this ploy, and seldom used corporal punishment.

The fourth saw Mr Granger "old Raindrop" whose speciality was music and conducted morning hymns at assembly, with the three senior classes in the hall while "old Newt" performed on the piano.

I can always see Newton sitting sideways on the cane chair, his legs being too long to get under the keyboard. On one occasion when the selected few of us were rehearsing for the school concert, Newton was so engrossed in his piano playing whilst we sang, his chair was moving close to the edge of the 6″ platform, on which the piano was placed. To our disgrace we were gleefully waiting – with breathless and heartless delight for him to topple over: which he did! Credit must be given to some, who grabbed him in time before he fell, it all helped the day along.

Whilst Grainger conducted the morning hymn session, beads of perspiration were always evident on his brow. He was invariably late in arriving on his push cycle. The dirty minds of little boys said they were quite sure he had sex every morning which subsequently caused his bad time-keeping. This observation brought sniggers from the worldly wise, and looks of bafflement from others. Some offered proof of this allegation by remarking that his wife had twins!

The next to crucify was Mr. Palmer, better known as "Dirty Dickie Palmer' or just Dirty Dicky. Another tall dark lanky man, clean shaven with black hair plastered with grease and parted directly in the middle, he wore pince-nez glasses which were extremely popular at that time, clad in black jacket and vest with pin striped trousers. This lank man suffered with a perpetual cold, and had an abominable habit of hanging his rather damp handkerchief on the large iron fire guard. Whilst watching the steam from the soaked cloth, I often wondered why he did not bring a larger supply of what we universally called "Snot Rags". This peculiar character delighted in confiscating boys sweets when the unsuspecting culprit was caught surreptitiously chewing. He then helped himself to the major portion of these before returning them after school. My most vivid recollection was after taking my packet of locust* beans he returned a much reduced number saying he would, "retain the rest as punishment". Later in the week he requested me "to purchase some for his children" and proffered one 1d! I doubt if his children even saw the beans, at least not the one I retained in retaliation.

Mr. Tremayne, or "Tubby Tremayne", was a jolly little robust ginger haired military looking person with moustache to match. He was, in fact, the first to enter the forces during 1st world war and returned when on leave resplendent in a Major's uniform. I rather imagined he was a Territorial

---

*Locust beans were cheap and popular with children, consisting of a dried brown bean pod, very sugary, and quite often containing maggots. These were an accepted risk, and added flavour.

before the war. I had little knowledge of him owing to his absence during that terrible conflict.

Mr. Kay next, quite nondescript, and lastly Mr. Hobling, naturally called "Oblong". Most of this bunch saw service except Ridler, Oblong and Granger. Consequently lady teachers were introduced! Such a revolution, which caused more excitement and gossip, than the war itself.

The most loved among the staff was the diminutive caretaker "Daddy Webber" all of 5' and a bit. Jolly and hard working, always in a hurry and never in the doldrums. His task was formidable, ranging from keeping the huge iron fires, one in each classroom, and two in the hall, replenished with coal. Plus the cleaning of the school which included the clearing up of vomit. This as previously stated, was quite a common sight. I always seem to remember him bustling about, carrying several wicker work paper baskets, looking like one of the seven dwarfs (namely Happy).

Whilst, alternatively, the most hated and feared individual was the dreaded "school board man", who was on the doorstep as soon as ones presence was missing from school. His tall forbidding appearance accentuated by his steel rimmed glasses mounting watery blue fish eyes, broken teeth partly hidden by a walrus moustache, slightly bent back, and stooping position, enhanced by a loping gait. You can envisage Mr. Scribe, complete with his writing board, and a bundle of absence notices, clipped to same. He would have made an excellent Gestapo agent, had he lived during that particular era. Sometimes he was known as the "Truant Man", but mainly he caught the malingerers, whose coughs and colds were as good as any excuse for a couple of days off.

Most public schools had their traditional tuck shop. We had several, in particular was "Hillaries" the greengrocer. This decrepid trading post was a source of amazement to me, with its meagre stock of fruit and veg which included a few pensioned off oranges. When in season a pitiful supply of chestnuts, these often purchased by ourselves when finances permitted. A ha'porth were often shared out, if one was lucky he may secure an eatable one, mine always seemed to be black or grey inside. At the front part of the shop was a huge pile of coal and an equally huge pair of scales. The scoop of which held almost 1cwt, plus bundles of firewood and coal blocks.

To obtain any benefit from the blocks, coal was necessary. They only caused a low red glow at the cost of a farthing or ha'penny each. Mother thought them uneconomical. The usual purchase of coal was 14 or 28 lbs, sometimes more, depending on the strength of the purchaser, and more important, the cash available. Some customers possessed a means of conveyance such as a home made barrow, consisting of an orange box, housed on a pair of cast off pram wheels. It was the desire of my life to possess one of these contraptions. But mother would not permit same to clutter the home. Often a pram or push chair was used, the latter then known as a "Mail Cart"* Why? It had no connection with the G.P.O. Nevertheless, it was generally termed as such.

Mrs Hillary was permanently pregnant, the family was only about seven to eight. I suspect she could have had regular miscarriages as a result of shovelling over the years. Many tons of coal must have been put into the highly placed scoop in the scales, coupled with handling the heavy weights, the largest being 56lbs.

I have rather less knowledge of Mr. Hillary, a rather weasly faced individual, who attended the outside trade, of hawking block salt, vinegar, hearth stone and whitening, on a pony and cart. At times he would vary his calling, by doing a quick removal job, at very short notice. It was quite common for a housewife to go shopping and casually look in a "House to let" which were in profusion and complete the incident by ordering a removal the next day. Consequently, if you perceived Hillary, with a few miserable sticks of furniture on board, you could be sure someone was seeking a change of residence. Also, in due course, some unfortunate tally-man was making a bad debt. Alternatively it could be the "Gipsy in 'em".

Some may wonder, why hearth stone and whitening? These were in demand by the scrupulous housewife, in a continuous war against muddy boots on the doorstep, and the latter for the hearth which was subjected to a constant fall of cinders from the open grate. Even during summer many houses had to light fires, as gas stoves were out of reach for many. For example, we in Beaconsfield did not possess such a luxury, not even gas lighting. Oil lamps were the order of the day.

Directly opposite Hillaries we perceive a very different type of shop "Crawfords" run by two dear old spinsters, who were robbed regularly by those who had criminal leanings. This shop sold all the good things, sweets cakes etc. The cakes were in open baskets on the counter and biscuits displayed in tins with glass fronts that opened at a touch. Also 1d Monsters that was gassy water known as Kola – Cream Soda or Lemonade. These drinks were in opposition to the famous R. Whites – Bateys – Rawlings and were only 1d per monster bottle, hence the name.

The purloining was achieved by crawling in on all fours and helping oneself whilst the dear old souls were in the back room. Should one get caught, excuses of all sorts were forthcoming such as "doing up one's

---

*Does anyone know?

bootlace", or "what's the time please," or "how much is so and so"? accompanied by a pained innocent expression. I was not perfect, and was too scared to participate in this crime, but it enthralled me to observe the event.

One contributory reason for sickness by several of the weaker pupils was possible bullying. These sub humans were always in evidence. I, too, had my share of fear of a bully – Eddie Warrington, whose brutal appearance was topped by a shaven head and a pock marked face. He considered himself virtually "cock o' the north". The shaven head was possibly to eliminate vermin and keep hairdressing expense to a minimum.

At one time I experienced being host to lice, bearing in mind during war time these horrible parasites were more in evidence, soldiers on leave being infected passing on their unfortunate condition. I spent many days kneeling in front of mother with a newspaper spread on her lap whilst she wielded a small tooth comb. She caught the parasites in the close mesh, followed by a wash in disinfectant.

There was little crime compared with to-day, which made the "Great Bakehouse Robbery" an exciting event. This was perpetrated by the Herring gang. The scene was "Richardsons the Bakers" at the top of Beaconsfield Road. There was an outside wooden staircase leading to a first floor store to which access was made.

The shops below were bakers and corn chandlers, the latter has now gone out of existence. This type of store was fascinating with its bins of corn, maize, middlings, and bran plus sacks of dog biscuits, even hay and straw.

So many times was I sent for a "Peck of Middlings" to be mixed with boiled potato peelings, in the hope that our few scrawny chickens could be induced to supply the family with eggs. This attempt at farming broke out at intervals. Our crossbred fowls were so rarely fed on a balanced diet, and were housed in father's pathetic attempts in constructing a suitable draught proof hen house. As a result eggs became a surprise if or when they appeared.

Imagine the consternation when one morning Mr Richardson discovered his storeroom had been burgled. Entry had been made through a small window on the landing of the outside wooden stairs.

The local professional counterpart of Sherlock Holmes, known as "Tec Lee", was summoned to elucidate the daring crime, which had a curious factor, the only articles stolen were packets of dog biscuits!

However, solution was soon forthcoming, by the fact that a large section of Gamuel Road School pupils were enjoying the proceeds of the crime. These were generously handed out by the Bony Herring Gang. Such was the one and only burglary to my knowledge perpetrated by them, and that probably

Walthamstow Education Committee.

MEMORANDUM *from*

HEAD TEACHER,

Samuel Rd Boys' School,

Dec 19th 1918

To _____

Frank Murfet has been a Pupil in this School for nearly five & a half years. His attendance has been regular & punctual. His conduct exemplary. He is a steady diligent worker, & I have always found him honest & truthful

A. J. Withycombe
Headmaster

In Stand Ex VII
(Passed for Labour Certificate)

BOARD EDUCATION.
Form 146 (a).

SCHEDULE III.

School District of _Walthamstow_

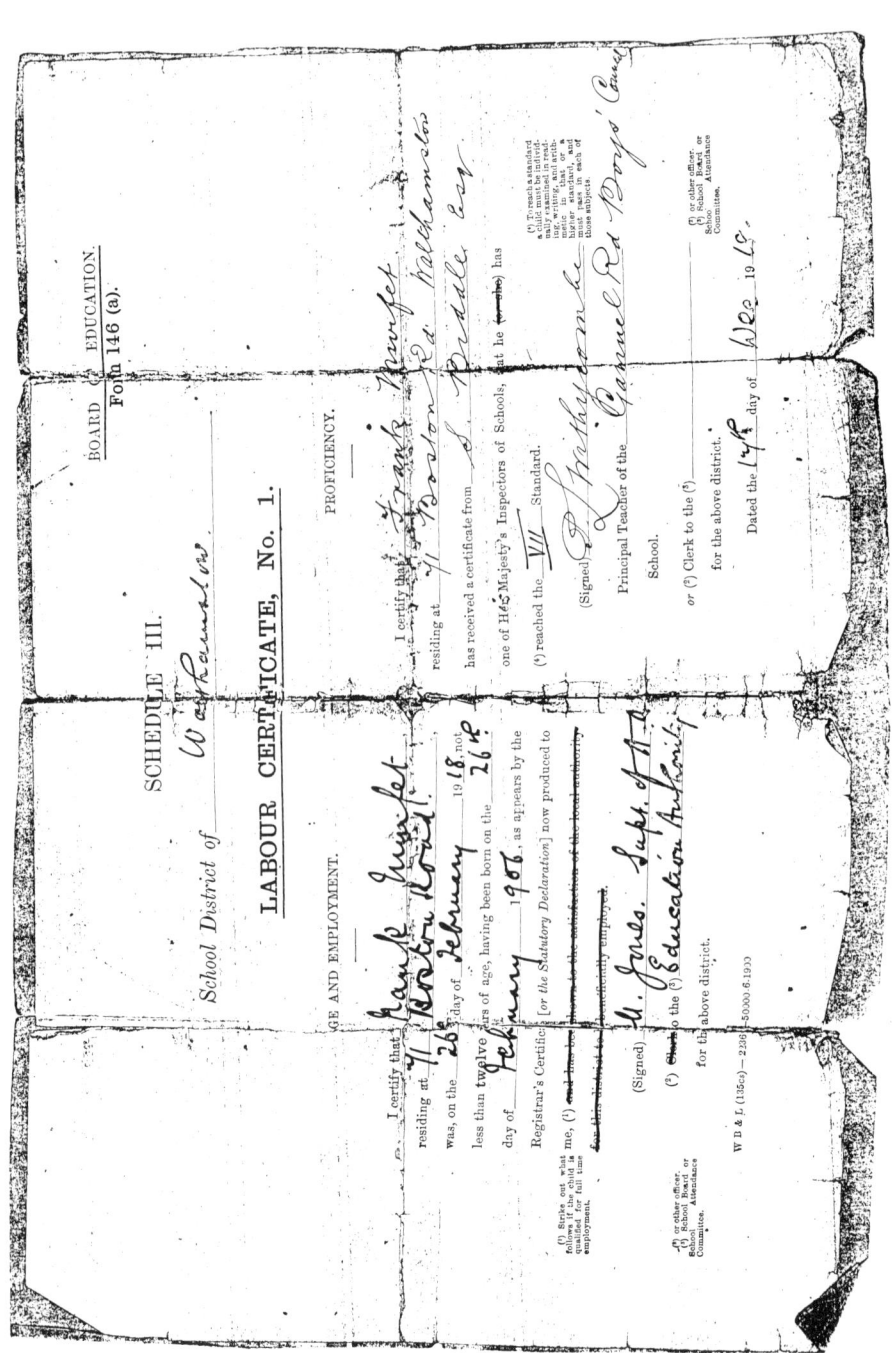

LABOUR CERTIFICATE, No. 1.

AGE AND EMPLOYMENT.

I certify that _Frank Munfet_ residing at _71 Renton Road_ was, on the _26_ day of _February_ 19_18_, not less than twelve years of age, having been born on the _26_ day of _February_ 1906, as appears by the Registrar's Certificate [or the Statutory Declaration] now produced to me, (¹) _and has been_ _____ is qualified for full time employment.

(Signed) _W. Jones, Supt. of N._
(⁴) _____ to the (³) _Education Authority_
for the above district.

W B & L (1350) — 2236 — 50000.6.1933

(¹) Strike out what follows if the child is qualified for full time employment.
(⁴) (²) or other officer. School Board or School Attendance Committee.

PROFICIENCY.

I certify that _Frank Munfet_ residing at _71 Renton Rd, Walthamstow_ has received a certificate from _S. Priddle Esq._ one of His Majesty's Inspectors of Schools, that he _____ has (⁴) reached the _VII_ Standard.

(Signed) _A. Nathycombe_
Principal Teacher of the _Canne Rd Boys' Council_ School.
or (²) Clerk to the (³) _____
for the above district.

Dated the _14th_ day of _June_ 19_19_.

(⁴) To reach a standard a child must be individually examined in reading, writing, and arithmetic in that, or a higher standard, and must pass in each of those subjects
(²) or other officer. School Board or School Attendance Committee.

This certificate was the last of its kind issued by the Board of Education to pupils who had achieved the limit of education by the school in question. They were at liberty to leave if employment had been obtained, or alternatively, sit for examination for entry to "The George Monoux School".

out of hunger. This of course was instrumental in causing the elder brother to be sent to an approved school, as previously mentioned. When he was eventually released, "Old Witty" made every effort to assist in finding him a respectable job. The fact that the spoils were handed out in the most generous manner and believe it or not were masticated by many whose teeth must have been exceptionally strong, the stomach equally so. Though the biscuits were tough, as far as the Harris's were concerned, it was something to eat!

Opposite the school, was a pitiful piece of grassland which was surrounded by railings, referred to by us as "The Reck", but named Queens Road Recreation Ground. It consisted of a patch of grass surrounded by an asphalt path extending to a hard baked garden of stunted shrubs, and unclimbable poplar trees. A dark marble drinking fountain, stood in an enclosed space. Two shallow iron cups, secured by an iron chain, strong enough for the prison chain gang. To drink from these, one tempted fate, or took a risk of contracting impetigo, a common ailment. Ridlers pupils were permitted to use "The Reck" during playtime. The superior feeling when leaving the confines of the playground under the envious eyes of those less fortunate, almost compensated us for the martinet discipline we endured. The fly in the ointment was the keeper known as "The Dotchy". He held many in terror, being the nearest to the Frankenstein monster, except he lacked the bolt in his neck. We were the ones to bolt, when he appeared on the horizon. The sight of his burly frame, with a red fire cracked face, large mottled nose, and a staring glass eye, which dwarfed its counterpart, put Cyclops in the shade. He was never without his iron spiked paper picker, waving it dangerously while he bellowed, "we spoilt his grass" or "made too much noise". He also barred ball games. He was best suited as a prison warder and after receiving a cuff from him, I avoided "The Reck" for weeks.

Queens Road, which bordered the farther end of this pitiful playground, was one of the first roads in the town to be tarred. The arrival of the tar pots and mobile boilers, with their Stephenson's Rocket funnels, accompanied by the ever exciting steam roller, drew enormous attraction. This was of further interest when the roller extended its powerful three pronged fork into the surface of the road and proceeded to tear it apart. Through this new innovation, the council unwittingly introduced a new kind of sport to the ever enterprising minds of the schoolboys. They discovered on hot days they could manufacture "balls of tar" from the road itself. A solid mass of a black gritty mess was moulded into a sphere, which played havoc with the hands and clothes of the miscreants. This surface was used as an experiment and was completed on the lower end of Queen's Road only. Perhaps it was as well. Before long, indiscriminate holes appeared on the spongy surface as a result of this new piece of mischief.

My schooldays inevitably came to an end with an unknown future in store. It was not long after I had entered a new phase in life that I realised schooldays were not so bad after all.

CHAPTER 6

Trams

WALTHAMSTOW was governed up to 1906 by a local board, from that date it became an Urban District Council. From 1905 it possessed its own electric tramway system, proudly launched as "The Walthamstow Light Railways". I had a deep sense of pride for this nondescript town, which was equally shared with this fleet of clattering monsters. They were the only form of public transport from Markhouse Road to Higham Hill, and Ferry Lane to the Napier Arms. The Bakers Arms to Chingford route was shared with omnibuses, and in later years with the Leyton and LCC trams.

I read with peculiar childish awe the name of Chas Murray, General Manager imprinted on each tram, and imagined him a benign and all important person. Although I do not hold him responsible, I was unaware that inspectors wages were £1.15.0 per week, clerks £1.10.0, drivers and conductors £1. 8. 6d, and cleaners £1.8.0. These magnificent salaries required a 60 hour week. A prospective driver had to learn in his own time. Incidental fines at court for overloading a tram was borne by the conductor costing approximately 10/-. In one case 87 persons were carried instead of the regulation 52. In February 1910 a child was born in a tram. A doctor was called by the conductor. The doctor on completing his task forwarded his account to the council, who promptly replied "They were not responsible for the event"!

I have yet to learn of an event even approaching the one which involved a tram in Chingford Road, on the fatal morning of Saturday the 23rd of January 1909. In spite of the passing of time, "The Tottenham Outrage" as it was reported, bears resemblance to crimes of to-day. During this period, Britain was receiving many immigrants from Russia. These included a number of revolutionary types, who were involved in that country's turbulent affairs. Among them were two Latvian anarchists, namely Paul Hefield and Jacob Lapidus. To acquire funds for their cause, they held up a wage clerk in Chestnut Road, Tottenham taking the sum of eighty pounds, equivalent now to at least two thousand. A bloody chase ensued which lasted over two hours. At one period a Walthamstow tram was held up by the two gunmen, near to where the Stadium now stands. The driver of the tram, a Mr Joseph Slow, promptly acted in complete opposition to his name, by scooting up the stairs, and who can blame him. The bandits smashed the locked door to the driving platform, forcing the conductor to drive at gun point, while a terrified lady passenger and her young family cowered on the floor of the madly careering tram. Meanwhile shots were exchanged by pursuing police in another commandeered tram. The villains then leaped from the tram to claim a milk cart which subsequently overturned. A further horse and cart was appropriated, and finally the miscreants separated. One attempted suicide, which failed. He died three weeks later in the Prince of Wales Hospital, Tottenham. The second was holed up in an isolated cottage, the occupant of which was in a state of abject terror. Lapidus was finally killed by a policeman, and thus ended the astounding affair, which cost the lives of Pc Tyler and a boy of 10, Ralph Joycelen, plus *sixteen* persons wounded. The stolen cash was never recovered.

This astounding episode in the lifetime of our light railways made national news for weeks, and spoken about for years. It was on par with the Sidney Street seige occuring later*. My age at that time was just over two years, but the affair was dramatically recounted to me by my parents, many times, years after.

The three routes used were in the main a single track variety which occasionally divided into a loop line, enabling the passing of each monster. Consequently one of the regular daily occurrences was to observe two trams meeting at a bend on the same track, whilst the drivers had a heated altercation as to who was to reverse to the nearest loop line.

Later, an automatic signalling system was installed which made no difference whatever! So we still enjoyed the periodical "punch-ups" whilst the patient passengers awaited the outcome. Things were taken so philosophically those days!

Another more rare, but far more amusing event was when a tram arrived at the terminus where one line divided into two sets, sometimes the front bogey wheels would run up one track and the rear four would decide to go on the other, result being, the tram was left broadside across the road. This brought a problem to the driver and amusement to the public.

There were two types of trams, one with four fixed wheels and another of

---

*Sidney Street: Two years after the Tottenham affair on the 3 January 1911, a further outrage, which drew more publicity occurred at 100 Sidney Street. Seventeen nights earlier, police were confronted by armed burglars, which was finalised by two anarchists being besieged for seven hours, at the address mentioned. This battle cost the lives of three policeman, and the two immigrant felons.

Winston Churchill, then Home Secretary was on the scene and directed operations. In all, two thousand rounds of ammunition were used, two contingents of Scots Guards, several fire engines, two thirteen pounder guns with limbers with twenty rounds (not used) plus many police, and nurses from The London Hospital. The lives of three brave policeman were lost. The two felons perished in the conflagration of the house. See Colin Roger's book "The Battle of Stepney" published by Robert Hale Ltd.

eight. Each set of four worked on a swivel from the centre. These were purchased secondhand from a very hilly district and subsequently were rather low geared and so created a terrific din giving the impression of a great speed, although only travelling at about ten miles per hour. It was the long eight wheelers which often got into the disjointed positions as previously mentioned. The four wheel variety being fixed introduced another type of problem.

For example, when rounding acute bends, of which there were many, the tram was only kept on the line by the flange on the iron wheels and so created a deafening screech when negotiating these curves. Often when the curves were taken at a break neck speed of eight miles per hour or more, the monster sometimes left the rails with complete abandon, coupled with a sense of freedom. On occasions it sometimes released its conductor pole from the overhead power cable, leaving it in ecstasy, pointing vertically and swinging to and fro. As you can imagine these were quite exciting moments.

I was once a passenger when the tram decided to release itself from the bondage of the rails, but retain its marriage with the overhead power. We were hastily warned by the conductor to "Keep your seats. Don't touch the handrails, they are alive with electricity".

We sat in trepidation while he went about his well rehearsed part, including the release of the pole. After the tram had been coaxed back to the rails, he proceeded to reintroduce the trolley to the overhead wire. This was achieved by holding a rope attached to the pole, which was held in position by an extremely strong spring. The wonderful show of flashes that accompanied this feat dwarfed Crystal Palace Firework Display and the language of the conductor was equivalently colourful.

This task required skill, strength and good eyesight. The near misses caused the flashes, while the ironic cheers of the heartless passengers did not improve the conductor's temper.

It is well to compare again the employment conditions of the driver and conductor of these monsters to the present day, even though the period is not all that long ago. For instance it was a common sight to observe the conductor leap from his exposed platform, while the tram was in motion, and almost gallop to various coffee shops to collect a pre-arranged jug of tea. He would then hurriedly return to his chariot-like platform swinging aboard with expertise. He would then proceed to unwrap his loving wife's sandwiches, partake his lunch whilst the tram carried on its merry journey. Their counterparts of to-day would possibly throw up their hands in horror with the "Everybody out" battlecry if they had had to tolerate this ulcer prone meal.

When I remind you that this section of the community were at the mercy of rain, hail, snow and often fog, it is to their credit they never cancelled the service, however bad the elements, even fog, at any time. Often the conductor of a General Omnibus who was similarly exposed would walk in front of the old 'B' type bus, and so assist the driver in his hazardous task of piloting the bus, to the various destinations. Lea Bridge Road was one of the most notorious spots for London's pea soupers.

There was a family atmosphere between passengers and conductors. The majority of conductors were most cheerful and in many cases entertaining. One in particular when calling out at various stops would make a humorous remark (this in itself is unknown to-day). On arriving at the River Lea Bridge one Wag would sing out that name, and follow it up by singing the popular hymn "Shall we gather at the River". He particularly had some witty remark and a quip for each stop. It was commonplace to see the driver of the omnibus with his own cushion and blanket. He being accompanied by his conductor also carrying his tin box holding the punching machine and tickets under one arm. He would not be without the inevitable blue enamel can with a cup that fitted at the top for the life giving tea, obtained by the same method as their tram counterparts.

Although the omnibus shook one to pieces, owing to the lack of suspension, aided by solid tyres, they had more warmth and intimacy than the tram, also less frequent stops. They were quicker travel though not too easy to read a newspaper – rather like attempting same, whilst attached to a vibrating machine.

Many elder persons did not take kindly to the "stinking petrol bus", but as cold weather approached, the warmth of these in contrast to the draughty tram, with its hard seats, proved irresistable.

Although I have mentioned the friendly atmosphere between passengers and staff, there were occasions, especially during rush hours, that free for all crushes existed. No person queued, it was survival of the fittest, with no holds barred. Once on board, it was "sod you Jack, I'm all-right". At the advent of the bye-law restricting the number of persons standing, and the queue habit formed, this uncivilised behaviour ended.

The demise of the trams in most towns resulted in the removal of the dangerous sunken rails. The replacement by the trolleybus introduced another hazard, crocodile traffic congestion. With the extremely fast acceleration of these comfortable vehicles, the public soon discovered they could not nonchalantly swing aboad very easily as it moved away from a stationary position. It was also rather fruitless to run and try to catch it when in motion, unless of course you were an expert sprinter in the Olympic class.

For a while everyone enjoyed the clean quiet mode of transport which was later replaced with diesel fumed juggernauts resulting in noise, stink and pollution with an equal amount of congestion. The so called march of progress is never without its attendant problems.

CHAPTER 7

A Unique Journey

I WAS six years old when I first experienced the most exciting journey of my life which was the forerunner of many similar.

When mother wished to visit her stepmother in Sawbridgeworth – a small, extremely pretty historical settlement formally recorded in Domesday Book as "Sabrixteworde", approx 29 miles from London, which has since been developed, but still retains some of its old charm – she would arrange by post to meet Uncle George (called Jim) at "Bakers Arms", Leyton. The simple explanation of this apparent peculiar arrangement was that he was one of the few remaining hay waggoners that made the regular journey from Sawbridgeworth to the Haymarket, London. On his return journey we would rendezvous as arranged. After usual greetings he would lift me up to deposit me in the wagon among the corn smelling dusty sacks. Mother would kiss us both farewell with the admonishment to "behave myself" and to her brother who was, by the way, a batchelor, "to please take care of that cough". He in return would reply in that typical Essex-cum-Hertfordshire dialect, "Oim aright Mary see you on Sa'urday". I would be thrilled with anticipation of the adventurous journey ahead. In due course mother followed on by train at the weekend. Her stepmother made a hard living as laundry woman to the elite and her end product was immaculate, professionally starched, ironed and packed in large wicker baskets for personal delivery.

By late mid-day, we would arrive at the "Fox and Hounds", Epping Road, which stood quite adjacent to the "Wakes Arms" (both of these hostelries are now demolished). The site of the former is now a gaudy petrol station. The ruins of the "Wakes Arms" is a sad reminder of its days of glory when it was voted as country headquarters of the Walthamstow Motor Club and a popular rendezvous of repute, to all lovers of the then, open road.

It was at this stage "Jumbo", a magnificent, and slow plodding shire horse was released from its harness and allowed to graze in the adjoining field, while the waggoners sat in the tap room, with the ever ready bread, cheese and onions, not forgetting "McMullens Fine Ales", which could be purchased for 2d per pint or 4d* per quart, better known as a "pot". It was the custom to call for this measure, and then proceed to hand it round to all

---

*McMullens Brewery was founded in 1827. The present one is built on the site of three wells, providing the water for the brews. It's well known ale cost fifty four shillings per barrel in 1915 i.e. 36 gallons. The business remains the only family brewers left in Hertford.

his fellow waggoners, who in turn would take a quaff. This gesture was made by all, as and when they arrived, and was a custom now lost in time. Mother had a marked revulsion of this habit, whenever present at the ritual when performed at "The George the Fourth" in Sawbridgeworth, even though females were not included in the "initiation".

I was allowed to sit with the adult company and was referred to as "Jim's little owd boy" – "who could sing a good song". After demolishing my prepared fare, and being supplied with free lemonade from the landlord, I needed little persuasion to render the popular song in fashion to the most appreciative audience.

Without knowing, I became a "professional" as a collection of coppers was made despite mild protests from Uncle Jim. The request for "I'm Forever Blowing Bubbles" was their favourite. On subsequent trips I was given strict instructions to refuse the proffered money and the admonishment from mother of "what will people think" ringing in my ears. From then on, when mother was present, my reward was relegated to an arrowroot biscuit. These large luxury's were always displayed in a glass jar, on the counter at one farthing each and are now a rare object. I had returned to the amateur status.

To watch the reclaiming of Jumbo, who usually had passed her motion while grazing, always brought a glow of satisfaction in Uncle Jim's pale blue watery eyes and the remark "ah that dun er t' world o good" was in keeping with his thought and kindness to his charge. The animal was, in fact, the mainspring of his life as well as his livelihood.

He would harness up and be off after this splendid interval and make treks for that final stage, which was always the most exciting. I cannot remember the actual time taken on the second leg, but it was always dark long before Sawbridgeworth was reached and Uncle Jim and I were deep in the arms of Morpheus quite soon after leaving the "Fox and Hounds". McMullens ale played no small part in this somnolent state, although it must be remembered, sleep could only be had when possible during this two day journey. Fortunately Jumbo needed no pilot or even a lamp, he acted as both, and stopped at Clay Lane, now called West Road, without a word of command. I venture to add, if we had not awakened at this stage he would have aroused us by discharging air through his nostrils, or his rear, which from my experience is not an uncommon habit with the equinine family. I was soon wide awake and assisted down with my well-worn attaché case containing my requirements, plus half a pound of "Strutts" mixed rock from that popular unique sweet manufacturing family situated in Markhouse Road, Walthamstow. To arrive without this regular gift would have been unforgivable and so in pitch darkness I would run the last hundred yards to

Seated myself. Front row: Grandmother Taylor, Mother, her brother Uncle Jim, the waggoner's dog. Back row: friends. Extreme back: driver of "Sheen".

grandmother's detached cottage No. 17 which still stands to-day, but bereft of its rural atmosphere and extensive garden as I knew it.

Grandmother, I may add, was not exactly of the story book variety. She was tall, strongly built and of typical tuetonic appearance. Her grey hair held flat and parted in the middle, steel rimmed glasses, from which two grey eyes peered not unkindly and were enhanced by crinkles on each side. A flat squared jawed face signified a great strength of character. Apparently, in her youth she had married my real grandfather and had taken on the responsibility of his motherless family of four girls and two boys, and had been more strict than usual, which may have been necessary.

After the demise of grandfather, she married again and became Mrs. Taylor. She had a brother who resided nearby, whom I referred to as "Uncle" Harry. His dour nature did not help in his somewhat indifferent attitude toward myself, having of course no real relationship ties. Nevertheless he created a childish admiration on my impressionable mind, owing to his calling: He was "second engineer" on a "Sheen"! Being interpreted in basic English, he assisted in driving a traction engine! This clanking piece of machinery towed a threshing machine in Autumn, and a twelve bladed plough in winter. The contracting farmer would loan these out for cultivation or threshing. Two men were in charge when travelling at a full speed of five miles per hour. The "Captain" handled the steering, which required countless turns of the geared wheel, which controlled the massive chains to turn the iron front wheels, while Uncle Harry would stand like a sentinal with his hand on a gigantic hand brake. His grim intense expression of concentration when on the move was almost frightening.

When set for ploughing, a second "Sheen" was placed at the opposite end of the field, while the plough using six blades was attached by a cable to a revolving drum under the belly of the "Sheen". The plough was then drawn across the field in the same manner by a second engine. When six furrows had been completed, the plough shears were raised allowing the other opposite six to be dropped. This required both machines to move forward a few feet, thus enabling the plough to make a return journey. This method was considered a major step forward from the twin horse drawn plough, although I should imagine costly. The traction engine for driving the threshing machine in the Autumn which was more colourful to watch, but extremely dusty for those employed at the task.

I have vague recollections of Mr. Taylor, a fairly small man who was a good deal older than his wife and spent best part of his time in the corner armchair wearing a small blue apron, which always appeared covered in ash from his well-worn briar pipe. Mother's jocularity, which increased when released

Box completely filled with stones.

Facsimile of grandmother's stone box mangle.

from household worries, was at times embarrassing; she would lift his mini apron with her umbrella whilst he was seated and enquire "what had he got under there?" This brought a frown of disapproval from Mrs. Taylor and a meaning glance towards my direction.

At the side of this house was a single-storey room housing the mangle. It was not the type you may envisage. This ponderous construction consisted of a large wooden box, filled with stones. This was supported on a heavily polished platform, with rails on the two longer sides, leaving the two ends open. On one side was a huge iron wheel to which a chain was connected to a cog wheel, which permitted the contraption to move backwards and forwards on two heavy wooden rollers. These would press the sheets and blankets to perfection and it was my task to turn this "infernal machine" whilst Mrs. Taylor prepared the next subject. It was required of me to assist by turning the huge wheel of this typical Victorian invention while Gran Taylor spread and changed the blankets etc. This task was most enjoyable to me, especially as it terminated in an evening's visit to the "The Cinema" – a treat beyond all understanding to the present generation. After tea on Fridays, grandmother Taylor would bustle around with the usual remark "We'ed best be a startin, the owd engines a going". The latter was a noisy donkey engine which drove the dynamo for the power to make this recent commercial enterprise of "moving pictures" possible. Although quite a distance away, the "chug chug" could be heard in the still air, enhanced by the fact no buildings obstructed the waves, and no extraneous noises impeded the welcome sound.

Our hurried arrival was sometimes after the single night's performance had just started. This meant the young girl usherette was disturbed from her chair, having contentedly settled to watch the show. The beam from her bullseye lantern showed annoyed faces of the audience, distracted by our belated arrival. When recognised these often turned to smiles and pleasant replies to Granny's abject apologies. After watching Pearl White being thrown from a cliff which, after all, made quite a diversion from being tied to the railway line, we joined in the laughter induced by "Pimple" Fatty Arbuckle or Billie Ritchie, these being only three of the well-known funny men. After standing respectfully to the tune of God Save the King, rendered with fervour on the tinny piano, we emerged from the semi-darkness to the pitch black of the passage leading to the main road. Within a short time we were in the dimly lit tap-room at the rear of "The Gate" public house. Here a flagstone room housing the whole stock of beer in wooden casks was set against the wall. A rough table and form was provided for those women who imbibed in a glass of stout in complete isolation from the public bar, and away from the lecherous eyes of the male customers. This final abandonment and gossip with a cronie or two was a just reward for a hard weeks work and in preparation for delivery next day by hand cart with the impeccably laundered contents laid out in various whicker baskets destined for the elite of Sawbridgeworth. Among which were Dr Collins of the "Red House", Dr. Burton and the Pykes in Pishiobury Park*. The approach was made at the tradesmen's entrance, to be met by the lace capped maid, usually a bovine looking girl sometimes not a great deal older than myself. This task was my ultimate delight and occasionally a copper was earned!

On Saturday mornings, prior to mother's arrival, it was a thrill of a lifetime to walk to Sawbridgeworth Station, served by the Great Eastern Railway. Its bare boarded booking hall with the iron weighing machine for goods in transit was my first attraction – a brace of pheasants or pairs of wild rabbits were a common sight to be sent privately by rail. From there I tried every chocolate machine in the hope that the mechanism might be at fault and subsequently deliver the goods without payment. Once before this had occurred and therefore the chance of the miracle repeating itself was always in the offing. The 'clonk' of the signal by the level crossing warned of the approach of the fussy clanking train. After standing back and gazing in wonder as the engine rushed by, belching steam and smoke, I sought the rear end of the train to witness the dexterity of the porter-cum-signalman handling two milk churns at one and the same time. This was achieved by revolving them on their base at a dangerous angle by expert twists of each hand per churn.

While absorbed in this remarkable act, mother would appear, complete with feather festooned hat, dark blue braided coat and carrying the popular straw basket common to those days, one part being enclosed in the other and held together with a strap. From then on my feeling of complete freedom vanished.

A sequal to these events.
1. *Many years later, about 1975, I was in the vicinity carrying out insurance business and paused outside the house in which I had spent many happy hours.*

    I diplomatically informed the resident the reason of my interest. She very kindly invited me to view the house from the inside, of which I gladly took advantage. Gone were the flagstoned scullery or "back place" as was also the atmosphere. Modern alteration was in stark evidence. When I asked "what had happened to the box mangle?" I was stupified by the reply "Oh! we smashed that up and buried the iron work in the garden under what was the chicken run". It was like learning of the death of a friend. Later still I have

---

*Pishiobury House was reputed to be the one time residence of Anne Boleyn, having been acquired for her by Henry VIII.

observed a complete renovation and the single-storey mangle room has given birth to a floor above. I was again tempted to call, but considered the occupants privacy.

2. Next The Gate public house drew my nostalgic gaze. I found the only original feature left was its unique hanging sign of a five bar gate. The same I had read so often as a child still appears on this fine piece of carpentry:

*Stay traveller come in here
There's bread and cheese
and good old beer
A pipe you may take if you please
likewise a chair to sit at ease.*

I received a warm welcome from a busy but pleasant lady, attending her duties. Most of the patrons were at lunch absorbed in business conversation, each group oblivious to the other. The juke box had replaced the site of the shove ha'penny board, while a bar billiard table substituted the skittles. In place of the flagstone floor were luxurious carpets. No sawdust or spittoons were in sight, neither pipes as advertised. The trestles which once supported the skillful product of the coopers were no longer required. Metal containers of lager etc supplemented by CO_2 are now in fashion. The whole interior had been transformed as are so many hostelries of to-day, whether for better or worse is a matter of opinion. I wondered if the ghost of my uncle Jim Haines in company with his companions, who had wielded their wicked looking clasp knives merely to cut their bread and cheese, and maybe casually slit the belly of a wild rabbit, were looking down in envy on this motley crowd. There is one certain fact, they would not have been content with the size of the drinks in view. Nothing short of a pot (quart) would have sufficed them.

3. The cinema is now a Roman Catholic church surrounded by residential property. Resulting from the advent of the Kaiser's war, The King of Prussia, which saw fit to change its title to "The Kings Head" then approachable down a flight of steps, has been replaced by a characterless block of flats.

I was barely eight years of age during one of our many visits, when both mother and Gran Taylor decided to take a stroll to Wareside* some 9 or 10 miles distant. The intention was to visit an aunt of mother's, who was blind, and a widow. I will leave the trek to the imagination of the reader. Suffice to say we arrived in the afternoon, weary and exhausted, at least I was. The fortification of several cups of tea, from the ever ready supply at Aunt Polly's open range fire, in company with three beautiful new laid eggs, each from "across the road", soon worked wonders. Gossip prevailed until it was

---

*A village 2½ miles from Ware.

decided to catch the train from Mardock Station, the first one on the old Buntingford branch line. G.E.R.* A puff of smoke was visible from the cutting in Hogam Hill, the porter cum signalman appeared from his box, and breathlessly announced "we were at war with Germany". The telegraph had not long been installed. By coincidence, over four years later, I was within a few yards of this station walking from Ware Town. A horse and trap passed and the occupant shouted as he whipped his horse "war's over sonny". I would have preferred a lift, under the circumstances.

---

*This delightfully pretty branch was an early victim of the Beecham Axe, and so contributed to the congestion of the roads.

CHAPTER 8

Entertainment

ENTERTAINMENT in Walthamstow was varied and quite plentiful, ranging from variety theatre and cinema plus the High Street itself, although the latter deserves a separate chapter.

Outstanding was the Walthamstow Palace of Varieties, alas now demolished, once an imposing polished red brick building, boasting of two grand towers. The several highly polished doors, respendent with brass fittings opened up to the beautiful terrazzo floor of the foyer. On the left of the box office, a marble staircase led to the grand circle, and its well appointed bar. On the right of the foyer, a wide corridor guided you to the stalls, fauteuils and another lounge bar. The manager in evening dress and a Ruritanian garbed commissionaire were always on hand to greet their patrons. It was all so inviting and real music hall.

Until I reached the adult stage, I never aspired to enter these portals, although from an early age I saw many performances from the celestial heights of "The Gallery". Whoever was responsible for destroying this edifice may possibly be pardoned, because of economic circumstances, but never excused by replacing it with a faceless row of characterless shops. Friday night was the most exciting night for me. Around the age of 14–16, when funds permitted, I, with a crony or two, would line up with a none too select crowd awaiting with tense excitement for the narrow door situated at the rear of "the Palace" to open. Nearby was the entrance to the pit – but this cost 6d!

In both cases, the narrow entrance only permitted one to enter at a time and, to make doubly sure, a turnstile also had to be negotiated. Our entrance fee on these unforgettable nights was 3d. After paying this sum through a tiny grill to a man with the appearance of a prize-fighter, he handed over a large piece of metal with the remarkable resemblance of an iron cross with a hole in the middle. This was clutched in our hands whilst we tore up the seemingly endless circle of stone steps. It was characteristic of climbing the inside of a lighthouse, only far more grim and cold. Ultimately, they terminated at the gallery itself, so aptly named, where the iron cross was surrendered to a mountain of a man, with even more repulsive features than his counterpart who dished them out. He was the epitome of a sergeant major, complete with spiked moustache! The only way to escape his searching scrutiny was to emulate an innocent expression, as often used when passing through H.M. Customs on the green, with more than the permitted amount of liquor.

He was at enemies with the world. One then sat on the front tier – a plain high wooden step, the edge of which was reinforced by a two inches rough steel band which, incidentally, cut into the upper portion of one's legs, quite painfully. Your knees were hard pressed and restricted by the wall in front. This was about three feet high and was surmounted by two or three iron rails. Between these was placed an extremely strong wire mesh.

To ensure a clear view of the stage, one suffered what was almost housemaid's knee, if in the front row. It also necessitated straining high or stooping low to avoid the iron bar which surmounted the wire mesh and also obstructed a clear but slanting view of the stage.

By a way of diversion if you chose the second row, one always had the pleasure of wiping their boots on the person in front, a feat which was denied by those in the front row. Alternatively, the top seat of all could be more comfortable because of a straight wooden back of greasy matchboarding which made a barrier to the flat expanse behind it. This area boasted of a temperence bar, containing a crude but efficient counter serving such delicacies as eccles cakes, pastry, also the then famous Tottenham Cake. The last named consisted of a heavy two inch thick slice of plain cake, with a layer of icing mounted on the top. This indigestible comestible arrived in huge trays and was carved out whilst you waited, with positive accuracy by the hairy handed attendant, whose fingernails were in perpetual mourning.

The delicious eats were sometimes supplemented by the very popular cheese cakes not, I may add, of the American Variety. The English version was again a heavy tart filled with an even heavier dough, and topped with icing and shredded coconut. Sometimes it was heated and running in warm tasty grease, probably margarine. To wash these down, minerals were served in extremely heavy glass bottles containing a marble stopper, which was held in place by the pressure of gas. These unique bottles are now antique pieces. How I wish I had kept the number I have bought, instead of rolling them down the steps when the luckless soprano was exercising her vociferous rending of 'One fine day'.

These bottles made a continental klink, klink, klink as they fell from one step to the other and striking the metal strip aforementioned which boarded each stair. This pastime was more usually applied during the interval, and only surpassed by the front row occupants who delighted in dropping orange peel and paper bags on to the 'rich persons', in the grand circle or stalls. These innocent pastimes meant keeping a wary eye on the bouncer with the thick moustache.

A somewhat greedy youth lodged with us for a while, while completing his apprenticeship as a plumber. He almost excelled Billy Bunter's appetite. After partaking Tottenham cake, followed by gassy Rawlings mineral, he would top up with chips from "Bannisters High Street", where we all made a beeline after the show. Eating these from the newspaper was more enjoyable than a banquet at "The Ritz". Not being content with the stodge previously consumed, the pantry at home was raided for anything procurable. My parents had invariably retired. Usually bread and cheese and home made pickled onions were on the menu. The onions were contained in a stone jar. When the jar was finally drained of its contents we were appalled to see a much pickled forlorn mouse, beautifully preserved, and very dead, in the vinegar. We were most concerned, having eaten all the pickles intended for Christmas. Mother was always a one to 'prepare' for the future, or save for 'a rainy day'.

If ever I bought a new tie or shirt, or whatever, mother's advice was 'save it for Easter, or Christmas', or whatever event may be in the offing. Her reaction to the mouse incident was of concealed delight, plus the observation 'that's the result of being greedy'. She was correct in one instance, although I could not quite reconcile why a mouse intent on swimming in vinegar resulted in us being greedy!

The evenings brought the queues outside the Walthamstow Palace and also the Carlton Cinema, which was opposite. Both places exuded a fascinating and delightful atmosphere characteristic to each. The live shows offered old time favourites, and a traditional scene. The cinema had not reached complete sophistication, but had a fast growing following. Its audience included a good majority of couples of either sex who obviously enjoyed the privacy of the darkened hall, wherein some amazing experiments were performed.

The Carlton was the super cinema of that age, built in 1912 or thereabouts. It put to shame the smaller 'Picture Palaces' already in existence, but did not yet come up to the standard of the real super cinemas which put in an appearance during the 20s and 30s.

Some of the older cinemas, better known as flea pits, were much in evidence. The most notorious of these was the St. James Street Cinema, more popularly known as 'The Jameos'. Apart from its chequered career, there was at the back a milk yard housing many hand pushed milk barrows. This fact is borne out by myself, waiting outside the entrance at an early age, on a wet and darkened Saturday morning at 6am. The reason: to assist the milkman, who had kindly arranged with my mother to employ me as an assistant – or drudge. Consequently, here I was at this unearthly hour, waiting for my potential employer whilst being fascinated by the continuous stream of workmen, some going to work, others returning. All were converging on St. James Street Station. The two coffee stalls under the railway bridge, doing a roaring trade with steaming cups of tea etc. whilst trains rumbled overhead at regular intervals, coping with the demand – it was 2d workmens return before 7am, then 4d up to 8am. How often in later life did I literally gallop up those station stairs to catch the waiting train, puffing away as I was myself. Very often the gates were relentlessly slammed in my face by the grim impersonal porter. The curses he suffered from frustrated passengers while performing his safety precaution act were many.

Returning to 'The Jamoes', which changed hands with monotonous regularity and always displayed a notice advertising the fact it was 'under entirely new management'.

It was finally dubbed 'the Super Cinema'! Flagrantly an afront to the Trade Descriptions Act. The latest owners had invested in a few pots of paint and a clean up, with a couple of palm trees at the entrance, in an endeavour to invite patrons. Yes, this particular edifice had had a varied history, once as an auction and store rooms on the site which was previously a slaughter house. It was situated adjacent to St. James Street Station, then the G.E.R. Great Eastern Railway, with trains running every 15 minutes or thereabouts from Chingford to Liverpool Street City. Consequently, when viewing the films, one heard the trains rumbling in and out. The silent films of thundering cowboys were enhanced by the sound of steam engines and a slight tremor of the building. This, of course, added life to some films such as 'The Fall of Pompei' and the like.

These stirring epics were accompanied by a solitary piano, which for reasons I shall never know, was placed on a small balcony, situated in the middle of the side wall. This instrument was only accessible by one solitary iron fire escape type of staircase, attached to the said wall. The balcony was only large enough to house the piano and pianist. The music maker would patter up and down the stairs whenever it was necessary, either to change his music, have a tea break, or attend to the call of nature.

Such a weird arrangement I have never heard of, seen before, or since. It was quite unique. The close, stale atmosphere could not be ignored and was prevalent in all cinemas of that period, some more so than others. This one had an aroma of urine mixed with it. This was because some of the younger generation could not bear to miss one second of the "Exploits of Elaine" or the "Perils of Pauline", and so they surreptitiously peed on the floor rather than venture out to the cold and grim toilets.

This was mainly because of the possibility of being barred from returning to the hall, by being confronted by the commissionaire. He was resplendent in a secondhand uniform which fitted where it touched, and reminiscent of a retired Turkish Admiral. He kept a vigilant eye on the young patrons for reasons to be explained. He would appear suddenly, and remark in no uncertain terms, 'You've seen this programme son, now beat it!'

To qualify this action, it must be realised that the tiny convenience was situated in the foyer, and consequently one had to leave the hall, and after vacating the actual picture showing section, it was fatal – for most children.

It was quite common to see the programme twice or even more, and the attendant had second sight or sixth sense for picking out the culprits – hence the ejection. I on one occasion in a similar cinema was unceremoniously marched home by my sister, Ada.

Owing to my long absence, the family were concerned, and the eldest sister had been despatched to seek me out. Permission had been granted for her to enter the cinema. We could always be found in the front rows. My surprise, on looking up and seeing her was remarkable, after all I was only entering into the third performance.

An attendant would often be seen walking in front of the seats, and in the aisles, with a watering can containing diluted carbolic. He sprinkled the floor with this liquid and while performing this task he would remark 'I'll come round and cut your cocks off you buggers'.

The females were equal culprits in this act, of which he was either unaware, or lost for a suitable reprimand.

'The Princess Pavilion' situated in the High Street was on a slightly higher grade – very slightly! Its entrance was up a long wide alley. The cinema had been erected on an isolated piece of ground. Here was employed a deaf and dumb attendant who put the fear of God in me and the others. His unintelligible shrieks and growls had to be heard to be believed and were uttered to keep us in line in the alley and eventually usher us to the backless wooden forms in the front few rows. The fellow attendants and operator, meanwhile, were engrossed in a game of pontoon on a card table in the aisle. After an interminable period, or so it appeared to all, a spot of light appeared on the screen amid thunderous cheers from the excited audience. We knew now it would not be long before William S. Hart would be chasing the Indians.

Later 'The Markhouse Cinema' was erected on the Boundary Fields. Progress was being made, tip up seats were installed and revolving air vents introduced, resulting in a charge of 1½d being made as opposed to the others at 1d, providing you arrived before 4.30pm on Mondays. This meant a race against time by taking tea to school, in the form of slices of bread and jam. If surviving the temptation of eating this beforehand, it was gobbled while we were being enthralled, watching 'Bronco Billie' easily dispose of the bank robbers, while he remained unscathed, although outnumbered six to one.

Such excitement and fun was the spice of life, and much appreciated. My earliest recollection of gaining entrance to a theatre when it meant almost fighting for it, was being taken to the Stratford Empire by 'Fat Aunt Ada'. She was childless and had great affection for her nephews, also shared by her husband (Uncle Bill), and she achieved great pleasure in indulging in this treat.

The gallery was superior to that of the Walthamstow Palace. It had a piece of red felt tucked along the wooden benches, and each patron was separated from his or her neighbour by a small half hoop of brass rail. This embellishment made a considerable impression on me. At this early period, prior to 1914, queues were unknown. One just arrived early and stood by the entrance, and as patrons arrived they congregated in a huge crowd forming a solid block of humanity. When the doors eventually opened, a concerted rush was made with much pushing and shoving, causing an unholy jam at the turnstile. Therefore Aunt Ada, being of ample proportions, was most successful in warding off the unruly mob, and shepherding myself, like a huge hen with her chick.

Sometimes the attendant would endeavour to organise some sort of order out of the chaos, with very little success. Strangely enough everyone took this scramble in their stride, and although recriminations ensued, no viciousness occurred. It eventually took a war to bring about orderly queues.

In later years, when the opposite sex were proving more attractive, it was the cinema that added to the attraction. When proposing 'a night out' it was without doubt 'The Queens' in Hoe Street which took priority.

This celebrated establishment boasted of bucket seats for two, situated in a few back rows with a curtain each side of the aisle making a perfect snogging haven in glorious seclusion. There were no awkward arm rests in between. In fact she could put her legs over your lap in perfect comfort.

This exciting experience could be brought for one shilling and six pence each. What value for money! One could lord it up for a few bob and the girl companion would be in no doubt of one's intentions if she consented to accompany you to this exclusive and without doubt favourite picture house. It does not need a great deal of imagination to realise one got his three shillings worth – and sometimes with interest.

Here the watering can with diluted disinfectant was not in evidence. In its place the attendant paraded the aisles with a fine spray syringe which exuded a cheap perfume and so created a harem like atmosphere which added spice and glamour to the evening's entertainment.

There was an instance when my face turned red in consternation during a performance. It happened when I was in company with a delightful female, who we shall call 'Annie', and whilst being extra flush and endeavouring to make an impression, I purchased a box of chocolates which mainly contained nuts and were of an obscure manufacture.

The lights as usual were switched on at the interval and accompanied by a heart rending scream from Annie. There were two or three pretty buxom maggots crawling up her blouse having escaped from the imprisonment of the box. All heads were turned in our direction, probably expecting my immediate ejection. However, with my diplomacy and Annie's sincere loyalty, we explained the cause to a much amused attendant. We were thankfully enveloped in darkness as the lights were lowered and peace reigned.

It was obvious the nuts were infected before being processed, or a blow fly had left its trade mark. The fact was they were there. Whatever the reason we both wondered how many were being digested in our respective stomachs.

There is no doubt many stories could be written of the bizarre incidents that have been enacted in the darkened halls of cinemas. The one which involved the extremely naive and greedy country youth of the pickled mouse fame typifies him. He once diffidently proposed a visit to the Carlton Cinema to a mutual girfriend of us both. Subsequently on a Saturday afternoon saw her about to settle comfortably, when he suddenly deposited a bunch of bananas in her lap, produced from a carrier bag, which incidently had intrigued her in the first place. They had obviously been purchased cheaply en route from the auctioneering stall in the High Street. Having overcome her shock on receiving such a number of these suggestive fruits, her controlled embarrassment later turned to merriment and relief, as he devoured all but one of his magnanimous gift.

'The Victoria Hall, Hoe Street' was the very first legitimate theatre in Walthamstow and the last to play the original melodrama. Now, on the same site, stands the Granada Cinema, built during the height of the season when real super cinemas were going up by the dozen all over England, i.e. late 1920-1930.

Even this truly magnificent building where, incidently, I worked as a plasterer, resembled a Spanish nobleman's residence, and a matching restaurant of equivalent beauty is now a shadow of its former self. Quantity has replaced quality, and its once splendid, waitress service restaurant is closed. In its heyday, four hourly programmes were usual. Two main features, three variety acts, a British Movietone News, and a full orchestra. In addition there would be a recital on the giant Wurlitzer Organ, that appeared and later disappeared into the bowels of the earth when ending its performance. This was often played by famous and popular organists.

The Granada Orchestra was truly magnificent, and billed as 'under the direction of Chas. Shadwell' – the same Charles Shadwell who became a well known band leader in later years. His display as a conductor was so energetic and effective that at times one expected him to fall backwards into the auditorium, especially when conducting the Overture 1812, which was a great favourite of his, and a joyous entertainment of ours. We always hoped, while in the throes of flinging his baton about in all directions and bending almost at an angle of 45 degrees backwards, he would finish up by toppling 'arse over head' as anticipated and voiced by the evil minded patrons. Fortunately for him this did not occur.

With such opposition, the smaller and original cinemas retaliated with cheaper seats and cups of tea handed out during the afternoon matinees. Had present day blue films been in vogue during this period, no doubt these would have been added to the repertoire, but the censor held sway and thankfully we were exempted from these pointless and boring exhibitions.

The old Victoria Hall, however, was the last haven of melodrama with an occasional change to variety, and still retained the atmosphere of the Edwardian age. Once during the First World War I was present during a dramatic scene, where a fight ensued, and one actor was struck and fell. His opponent knelt by his prostrate body and acclaimed in ringing tones 'My God he's dead'! Whereupon a voice from the audience shouted 'take his boots off'! Obviously the wag was a soldier on leave from France, the expression being commonplace in those war torn days when the action of relieving anyone who had no further use for his boots was an accepted fact.

I once managed to pass muster by gaining entrance to 'an outspoken play', so the play bills announced. 'For adults only' the caption read, which gave vivid impressions of torrid sex scenes. It was in fact an extremely mild approach to ordinary everyday problems, that to-day would go unnoticed. In one scene an erring daughter confessed to her mother, in a tremulous voice, 'I am going to have a baby'! From a women, seated right next to me, came an involuntary cry, in a voice choked with emotion 'bear up girl, bear up'! Such feeling, that even the actress had difficulty not to take a bow, as a tribute to her acting. Although the old hall did not achieve or compare with the Palace, sadly it succumbed earlier under the pressure of films, making way for the beautiful architectural grandeur of the Granada. Again, this in turn deteriorated to its sadness of the present day. Only a miracle can revive it now.

An entertainment which cannot be construed as entirely legitimate was that of the buskers, who were prolific in number and variety. The most unique of these were two separate individuals who worked in the trains from Chingford to Liverpool Street.

The third class carriages, in the early days, were bereft of the upper part of the partition. Consequently, on standing up, one had a clear view of the whole coach.

As the train left Liverpool Street, one was suddenly disturbed by the strains of a concertina, or sometimes the lively plucking of a banjo.

Either of these musicians would be seated in the middle compartment, hurrying through their repertoire, while their companion would hand round his cap, then hang over the partition on either side for further contributions. As soon as the next station was reached, they would scramble out in a feverish attempt to find another compartment and thus continue the act.

The concertina artiste was quite blind, accompanied by a small boy. The alacrity with which they made their exit and entry was as amazing, as it was hazardous. These events were mostly Fridays and Saturdays, when passengers moods were benign in view of the rewarding days for the weeks toil.

Jugglers, tap dancers, singers, musicians of all kinds would themselves line up to take their turn in entertaining a queue of patrons to cinema or theatre. It was extremely amusing to the patrons, when they all started to move quickly at the opening of the box office. The erstwhile performer would break off his act abruptly, and make frantic attempts to collect the coppers from a fast disappearing audience, frantically waving his cap under their noses whilst they were more concerned in gaining entrance rather than contributing to his welfare.

After the first world war, many demobbed soldiers formed small bands supported by female impersonators, with outrageous makeup and daring dresses.

A dance mat would be spread and a most entertaining performance would be enacted. Ten minutes of this, collection made, and away to the next street, followed by a trail of children.

Quips and gestures by the drag artistes created paroxysms of mirth from the housewives who would view from their respective front gardens. These troupes were very popular and worked the streets during the day, and the theatre queues at night. If a band was not available, a street organ would be the accompaniment.

'Splinters' and 'Soldiers in skirts' successful professional revues eminated from this street entertainment.

The cheapest and most versatile of entertainment was undoubtedly to be found in the High Street with its occupants on market days, which I have endeavoured to portray in the next chapter.

CHAPTER 9

The High Street

ERRANDS! The bane of my childhood, that had to be endured. Nevertheless it had its compensations, when I was requested "To pop up the High Street". This raucous market held a fascination to me, being the scene and centre of unique attractions. Its versatility increased at weekends, and on occasions the mile of stalls were in business until midnight. St James Street adjoining contributed to the trading although our light railways used this thoroughfare, and missed the stallholders by a hairs breadth. It was a miracle accidents did not occur daily, but by the grace of God, miracles were in evidence, aided by the alertness of the vendors. The number of naptha flares hanging from the stalls gave a yellow to orange illumination, and not a little warmth. It was itself a warning not to get too close to the fearsome flame, which created dancing shadows and a cheerful atmosphere, while the leaking kerosene with its attendant smell was accepted – it had to be!

These homely features ceased as soon as the first Zeppelin raid began and so the initial blackout was inaugurated. This characteristic flare was substituted by dim night lights, and flickering candles, placed in a box on the edge. The box front was covered by a transparent white paper showing enough light to give change. This barely illuminated the wares, so one had to buy almost on trust, so adding another of the many smaller miseries inflicted by the war.

However, war or peace, I haunted the High Street, listening open mouthed to the conglomeration of characters who were persuading and cajoling the shoppers to take advantage of the amazing bargains or cures on offer.

In spite of my mother's continued fault in forgetting some of her requirements, who would on my return casually remark "Oh just pop up the High Street again", with monotonous repetition I was not deterred from wandering off on my own on Saturday afternoons. It was then the market was at its best, and I free of any responsibility.

On these occasions, I possessed a few coppers from father and sisters. My pleasure was to watch, and later to ape the various "barkers", among which was my favourite ex Dr. Brown. This King Edward-like person, stood aloof, adorned in a frock coat, morning trousers and spats half covering his highly polished shoes. A resplendent gold chain and hunter spread across his waistcoat, which was consulted from time to time, with a professional air. Completing this spectacle was the adornment of a shiny silk topper, and a silver topped ebony walking stick. These played a significant part in enhancing his dignity. I revelled in re-enacting these characters, at various parties, until quite late in life. With due modesty we all inherited father's gift of mimicry.

He stood upright and very regal 5'6" supported by the said ebony walking stick and seriously listened to his son extolling the virtues of his astounding cures, while his pedantic expression was most impressive. By his side was a signwritten board referring to the authenticity of his previous status as a medical practitioner. Unfortunately, his son sadly lacked his father's demeanour, his looks or his diction. In fact he appeared exactly what he was – a street vendor.

He usually wore a brown suit and boots and spluttered rather than spoke, and also had a slight impediment in his speech. However, try and imagine this person with glaring eyes, starting his repertoire with "My farder – Dr. Brown – Ex. Dr. Brown, late surgeon to vy division of der Metropolitan Police". You will note he had difficulty in pronouncing "the". It sounded like 'D's, Rs and Ys were also peculiar to him. However, he continued "Who was struck from der Medical Vregister, as a result of doing a kindness to a young woman – who talked"! At this juncture, he would sweep his audience with a meaning look. Of his many cures, one was a cough candy. When recommending this, he held a slab in one hand, and with the other pointing to the medicant, would say "Diss ere contains de hoil of peppermint – der hoil of lavender – de hoil of hoar hound – de hoil of juniper", and several other "Hoils". His climatic remarks were "hif your little mite keeps you awake at night, and is racked with coughing – then put it in his little fist and let him suck it"! Each reference to the ingredients were accompanied by his eyes taking on a terrifying glare, and sweeping in a circle to the audience who stood in mute admiration.

Dr Brown appeared quite regularly, was a local resident and earned considerable respect. Occasionally we were visited by a Dr. Strong whose qualifications were suspect. He specialised in an aphrodisiac, Damianer! He attracted quite an audience by his outspoken and forthright approach to sex. At the time, this brought titulation and admiration from many and looks of disgust from the few. He was a tall immaculate person, dark and handsome, blessed with the deepest and richest of voices and was the epitome of sartorial elegance. Black coat, fawn vest, pin stripe trousers, crevette, black patent shoes, a monocle dangled from his immaculate collar. The single eye glass was occasionally used with a flourish, when reading out his testimonials. These were displayed in a seemingly careless way on his stall. A doubtful large diamond ring flashed, as he described his wares. His enriched voice was his fortune as on approaching his subject he would disdainfully remark "From disease I am immune", (a startling announcement), then, "I have here Damianer, culled from the mountains of Spain, blessed by the life giving sun". Remember Spain to us all, in those days, was as mysterious as the source of the Amazon. As much as the general public knew of most of Europe were the songs of that era, such as "If I catch Afonso", or "Lady of Spain I adore you" etc.

Dr Strong raises his right arm and points skywards on each mention of Damiana, whilst fixing his eye on likely male customers eagerly drinking in his rhetoric. "Damiana the herb of life, it makes you what you should be to your young wife". You could hear the gasps. "Damiana! It is energising and makes you immune from lassitude!" Men started feeling in their pockets. "Damiana!" and so on until he disposed of his red pills to a calculating male audience.

The young were left with the grand imagination of an illusion of repeating the sexual act for an indefinite period. The middle aged thought they would be able to repeat their honeymoon – and the elderly fervently hoped to make a comeback! Whilst Dr. Strong left, with increased wealth.

Whether the miraculous remedy worked or not, I was too young and innocent to find out, I can only say to me this speel left me with confused ideas. I was extremely naive, I would go so far as to say completely innocent, mainly by the complete and utter Victorian attitude of mother, and the extreme indifference of my father. Both had many good points, but sadly lacked in passing on the worldly education necessary.

Dr. Brown was a genuine ex MD. I cannot vouch for Dr. Strong's bona fides, but he was a well known "Market Practitioner" seen in Leather Lane, Holborn, and Tower Hill, later in life. There were however many fly by night quacks, who must have travelled extensively to market their useless remedies, as a repeat performance in the same market place would have been fatal.

One in particular, a black man, with heavy gold rings adorning his fingers, dressed extremely flashy. His English was broken but attractive. It was a rare sight to see a coloured person in those days.

This person sold tooth powder and displayed his excellent set of teeth as proof of his product. His opening remarks I remember quite well: "Ladies and Gentlemen, I are just arrived from de Gauld Coste of Sout-Aprica and I are brought wid me a toot powdah, made from de root ob de-" here an obscure name was used, "Say" "From de root ob de Oojah Tree – you notite mah teet am powah white" etc. I was fascinated by this rare spectacle who at the end of his convincing exhaltation, offered one box for 6d and one free.

I was so desirous of obtaining this rare tooth cleanser, I waited until the sales were over then diffidently approached him and apologetically asked if he would sell me one box for 3d which was all I possessed. With a furtive glance he accepted the proffered amount for the same and I departed joyfully. When informing mother of my bargain she immediately said "You have been caught silly boy, it's chalk"! She was as often quite correct.

I still, on occasions, fall for the five card trick from convincing salesmen. We all have our weak moments. Even as late as 1937, I fell for a delightful con trick. While wandering in Leather Lane, Holborn, with brother Arch, we were convinced by a salesman selling "Unbreakable china". We both purchased a quantity, after seeing this wizard skim the plates along the pavement. I was married at the time, and on arriving home, convincingly informed the wife we were now free of breakages, and to prove it skimmed a plate along our tiled hall. It broke into several pieces! My wife thought I had taken leave of my senses.

Later I learned brother Arch had superceded my effort by throwing two plates, in reckless abandon. Moral: "There is one born every minute".

A character of note and the most versatile, was a short chubby person with a moon face, untidy to a degree who sputtered over whatever he was selling owing to his lower lip protruding to an unusual extent. It was owing to this lip he was dubbed as "Lip Bert" and was never lost for words. He was a freelance barker employed by any stallholder who required his services. Whatever the wares it made not the slightest difference to "Lip Bert". His versatility was limitless. His best speciality was chocolates and sweets and when extolling the virtues of these would be astounding with his explosive expletives. Following his vivid description of the ingredients, his final verdict would be "Ere yar peepul choklits these are – not Sh—!"!. In his enthusiastic peroration, he would be spluttering all over his merchandise: at times uncovered! It was most surprising he was not aware that the public could quite see the distinction he made in describing the merchandise. Among the many traders was a superman. He did not make a public display of his strength knowingly, he merely sold rolls of lino and oilcloth in his shirt sleeves with a leather apron adorning him for obvious reasons. He had a magnificent lean frame and a leather wrist strap on both wrists. He lifted a whole roll of lino and held it across both arms in a horizontal position, whilst his partner supported the end of the roll and stood still while the strong man walked backwards. He would unroll the lino by bouncing it on his forearm, displaying its full pattern. While performing this prodigious act he continued his sales talk to the potential customers. The strain imposed was apparent, as he extolled the virtues of his merchandise. He would finally arrive at the price smacking the face of the lino with his right hand, whilst his left arm supported the full weight. Many times this feat was repeated, resulting in no sale, while sweat poured down his face even in winter. His lower jaw used to tremble which, I suspect now, was a nervous affliction, such a picture is hard to imagine. This Jewish gentleman's real name was Mr. Searl and correctly dubbed "The Lino King". The whole width of the road was used when displays were in progress and the large audience forming around took on the appearance of a circus ring. It was potentially a strong man act. He was a credit to his race.

Another lost sight today are the huge brass jockey scales highly polished with a comfortable armchair hanging from chains. The owner sat on a box at the opposite end, lifting tremendous iron 56lb weights and while watching the indicating needle in the centre would bawl out in stentorian tones 15 stone 10lbs 6ozs or whatever the customer weighed. It was of no use trying to keep a secret of ones weight as he bellowed it out to the whole world, and then presented one with confirmation on a slip of paper to prove it. All this for the price of one penny. I wonder what his daily takings amounted to?

This beautiful brass structure stood outside "Cardos", the old established boot and shoe emporium. Mr Cardo mainly catered for working mens heavy footwear with a variety of hob-nailed boots and even wooden soled clogs, reinforced by strips of iron on the soles and heels. This corn producing footwear was worn by many poor children who considered themselves fortunate, as indeed they were, as a few had no footwear at all. Opposite Cardos was Mr. Howards toy shop and the much publicised "Dolls Hospital". Here was a treasure house of toys, where envious eyes of children were always directed.

A screamingly humorous episode happened one Saturday afternoon. A character sold a patent glue, which stuck almost everything – at least that is what we were informed. This tall dark cadaverous man sported a drooping black moustache under which was seen two very white sharp teeth, reminiscent of a rat's incisors. He also possessed wicked flashing eyes, and an extraordinary nasal voice. Attired in a greasy black frock tailed, coat and equally dirty baggy trousers, terminating with a pair of scruffy boots of enormous size. His success in holding the audience was his voice and eyes.

On this particular occasion he persuaded a small boy to hold the lighted candle with which he warmed the toffee like substance. When the glue was well melted he smeared it on to a piece of wood which he joined to another. When it cooled he would dash it to the ground to prove the strength of his product. Whilst he made this repair he would hold the audience with a continuous spiel in his nasal tones, as follows: "It may be a corner of a table"

– pause – "It may be the corner of a side-board"! – Pause – "It may be the leg of a chair"! – Pause – "It may be a piece of a peearno"! – Pause – "I don't care!!, "You can smash it into a thousand pieces and it will not, I say, will not, come apart!" etc. (Whereupon the repaired piece of wood was dashed to the ground at the appropriate moment, adding a climax before making the sale.)

Now comes the "Pièce de Resistance" – You will have to envisage a small boy, wheedled from the audience, who was asked to hold the lighted candle, while the operation of melting the glue was in progress. This same innocent child rather respectably dressed, wearing a white scarf with silken tassels, which were fashionable in those days. This same small boy stood gazing into the hypnotic eyes of the glue purveyor, as if under his spell, whilst the candle caused the tassels to smoulder and eventually catch light. All unbeknowing to the candle bearer. Rather than distract the audience, especially as the glue seller was on his climatic finish, he continued his oration without batting an eyelid, while making frantic efforts to pat out the flames with his free hand. The boy remained entranced, totally unaware he was at the end of a fuse. Looking back on this, it was extremely amusing, but to describe the actions, with the mimicry of the voice, makes what many have remarked "A music hall sketch". The voice contributed mainly to the scene. On each "It may be etc" his left hand would pat the smouldering tassle in unison. It was only when both hands of the glue vendor were free, he could successfully complete his fire fighting act. The innocent victim suddenly became aware of his incendiarous position by throwing down the candle and assisting in the operation. By this time the audience were engulfed, not by fire but by merriment.

Such fun, such entertainment, such excitement, was all to be found in the High Street and all free!

The previously mentioned lino kings' pitch was in front of the old fire station which was operational in my youth. I gazed in awe at the glinting brass work and the steam boiler of the horse drawn fire engine, with the harness hanging over the shafts, ready for use. This vague recollection became more vivid when the inevitable change to motor occurred in the early part of the century when two new "commer motors" appeared followed by varied public comments. The brass helmets with the attendant gear were placed in full view of the public as were the firemen, who were always wearing their high leather boots, and glamorous uniform. Their presence at the doors, with the engines in the background, was an added attraction to the High Street – and also the opposite sex. The majority of the Brigade were ex sailors and who was to doubt the assumption that "all the nice girls love a sailor" according to Marie Lloyd or was it Florrie Ford?

Nearby was "Raphaels" the gown shop. Mrs. Raphael was invariably outside her premises making an imposing figure and clad in a creation, designed to attract attention. Any female who chanced to view the window display would immediately be cajoled and persuaded to enter "Under no obligation dear". A sale would be made, before the proverbial exclamation of Jack Robinson! Mrs Raphael was a commanding and extremely smart lady who possessed plenty of flesh to command. Her upright carriage with her right hand decorously placed on the upper part of her chest, disclosed by the square neck dress with the rings on view, would have put Mae West in the second division with regard to female attraction. Many alleged that she kept her money in her bosom, hence the position of her hand.

The past glories of the costermongers' barrows were the salad stalls. These piled high with water cress, tomatoes being inserted between the bunches – lettuce, cucumbers, radishes and the delectable bunches of spring onions. Heads of sweet smelling celery and above all the steaming hot beetroots cooked in the vendor's copper, no doubt after the weekly wash had previously been boiled, thus adding special flavour. Then, various fruits and vegetables only appeared when in season. Modern farming now can produce out of season and although this may please many, the pleasure of anticipation has gone, as also specialised shops. Supermarkets have transformed the art of shopping. We have to assume it as progress – I wonder!

Unless you had money to spare, you were not welcome to wander in "The Arcade" next door to the "Chequers". This dingy open-fronted hovel, held automatic machines "For amusement only", including "What the Butler Saw", "A Day at the Seaside" and the most daring of all – "A Night in Paris". If one caught a glimpse of two plump female legs, encased in horrible striped stockings coupled with a prodigiously proportioned bust, showing the tiniest bit of cleavage, that was the ultimate!

The gambling consisted of a ha'penny in the slot machine which produced one ball-bearing, which was hit by a spring trigger operated by ones thumb. The ball then went round and round a groove. When the momentum finished, it dropped in one of the six holes, showing "4 wins" and "2 losers". These holes were protected by pins, suffice to say the odds were cunningly arranged. To obtain a win was almost impossible, but should you be so successful, the reward was your ha'penny back and the ball returned. Eventually one always lost. I have never known a profit to be made on this momentous gamble. The younger generation were not welcome, if they were not spending money. In no short time I was often told to "Clear out" by the sleazy looking proprietor, who always reminded me of a character from Dickens. A slightly built weazel faced, under nourished, evil looking individual. He had a permanent cigarette end attached to his lower lip, appearing to be a built-in appendage. He slouched rather than walked and his permanent expression was that of an unemployed undertaker. Later in life I was tolerated, but by then the curious attraction had faded, I could never reconcile or forget the unpleasantness of weasel face, or the bare boarded dingy premises.

The toffee maker with a boiling pan of ingredients, the large flaring spirit stove, being pumped at intervals, producing a frightening jet of flame, and the manipulation of the huge "sausage of toffee" being pulled and twisted from a large hook was extremely interesting to observe. Nearby was the sarsaparilla distiller offering the health giving drink with its enriching qualities to the blood, at least so his testimonials claimed by being boldly displayed in wooden frames. These imposing certificates were headed by some obscure society of herbalists. All added spice and glamour to this street of never ending interest.

Prior to Lloyd George introducing sickness benefits in 1909, clubs for this contingency were popular among the poorer communities. They therefore continued to supplement the modest sickness payment, made under the new Government Act. Thus it was one of my many and never ending errands to pay father's "Sick Club" dues on Saturday evenings at "Conway Hall" attached to the church, then situated at the top of the High Street. The title of the club was *"Marsh Street Sick Mens Benefit Society" which always puzzled me until I learned of the reason. This trip occurred every three weeks, being the permitted period to be in arrears, before being fined 1d per share. Mother's gasps of surprise and remarks "time flies" always alerted me to the fact my evening trek was in the offing.

The only redeeming feature was to again view the bustle and glamour of the market which continued until late in the evening. Otherwise, the prospect of sitting in the dimly lit gaslight of the musty church hall, waiting interminably for the name of "Walker" to be called, was most boring indeed.To a young boy, who at times fell asleep and sometimes missed his turn, it was almost a nightmare. As one entered this typical church hall, which was the venue for all religious activities from Sunday School to Bible class studies its gloomy atmosphere was apparent. There were rows of hard wooden forms, and individual chairs, with the inevitable harmonium on which was a residue of well worn hymn books. Beyond this was a diminutive stage flanked by brown drab curtains reminiscent of old army blankets.

In front of the stage sat two elderly grey haired gentlemen, one being Mr.

---

*There were three churches built on this site, the last being erected in 1871. Marsh St became the High Street in 1882.

Gore of 62, Greenleaf Road, (Secretary), a name imprinted in my memory. So many times did I read it when on these irksome visits. The next initiation was to place the contribution book face down on an enormous pack of the same, being careful to avoid the inkpots on the green baize cloth.

The pale glow of the light supplied by the "Lea Bridge Gas Company" shed its full share on the shiny bald pate of the treasurer, whilst the rest of the hall was in semi darkness. Mr. Gore then proceeded to select the books in strict order and in a sonorous voice would call out "Mr. Walker", causing me to jump up with alacrity, unless otherwise asleep. In some cases, a member would leave the hall for a smoke and miss his turn, in which case the book was returned to the bottom of the pack. Arriving at the table, Mr. Gore would look up with an enquiring manner whilst I volunteered "Three weeks please", in the most subservient voice. The flat monotone would then spell out the message to the silent partner in charge of a massive ledger. "Mr. Walker No. 6484" eightpence", or whatever: having signed the book which was then handed to his partner, who in turn checked the entry with raised eyebrows. On some occasions a secret low toned conversation was held with Mr. Gore, which left me isolated with cap in hand feeling like that famous boy in history, being asked "when did you last see your father". Although I may have felt like him, I was not so sartorially as elegant as he. As beneficial as these clubs were the rules applying when on sick benefit were stringent. To enter a public house meant being struck off. To be caught outside home after permitted hours meant a fine, or worse. This was left to the discretion of the committee.†

To enforce the latter, sick visitors were appointed to visit or snoop, however one interpreted the call, without prior notice. There were several more bye-laws which now escape me.

A terrifying evening occurred when a visitor called one dark and dismal night, while father was claiming benefit for bronchitis while he was wicked enough to be out.

On this occasion mother had sensed who was at the door, it could only be the dreaded visitor. No one was expected. All the family were in! Father had the only other key – apart from the one that was attached to a string just inside the letter box. Frozen silence by all! A second knock – slightly louder, and a third – beads of perspiration on mother's brow – a dryness in all our throats. Had we all been on a charge for murder, the atmosphere could not be more stifling. Finally, steps fading away could be heard, even then no one

---

*Should any kind person still have an old membership book, the author would appreciate a sight of same for historical purposes. Communication to the publishers would receive appropriate attention.

dared to stir in case the inquisitor returned, or was hovering by the gate. Such was the fear of authority and the subsequent penalty that could result. The visitor returned the following night, father making quite sure he would be home and ready with his perfect alibi, "The family had gone to visit relations leaving him tucked up in bed with a hot water bottle and lemon water. Yes, I did hear the knock – it woke me up – I felt it foolish to leave a warm bed, etc." The experienced histrionics saved the situation, also the dire results of his crime in breaking the rules. Nevertheless, a much needed service was efficiently conducted by these worthwhile institutions. They served a need, and if any excess profit was made, a share out at Christmas was a welcome event.

It may be interesting to note these many sick clubs were used to administer the new state benefit introduced by law and were "approved" by legislation as were insurance companies, who also had a section known as "Approved Societies" thus reducing the cost of administration. Obviously no special departments were necessary as "Sick Clubs" and "The State Panel Benefits" were interwoven, and the administration was already in being.

As soon as approved societies were disbanded in 1948 and the present day administration took over, so higher costs were inevitable.

About 10 p.m. the traders are hurriedly disposing of the perishable residue of their wares at knock out prices. The butchers are auctioning bloody joints of meat and the fried fish shops are preparing for a rush when the second house of the "Palace" and "Carlton" discharge their bleary eyed patrons. Some with higher sense of values will visit the jovial Mr. Watcham (Mr. Watcham was the initial President of the first Walthamstow Motor Club, founded by myself and several keen motorcyclists. He was proprietor of "The Palace Tea Rooms". A jovial cherubic faced man with a mop of wavy black hair, matched by a decorous moustache of the same colour. His generous portions of egg and chips with roll and butter and a real cup of tea would set you back 9d. A few of the night owls may wander round to Hoe Street Station or further down the High Street where at either venue the popular sight of a coffee stall appears as if by magic. At each stall one would see a damp tea stained cloth covering an enormous brown enamel teapot, from which a liquid looking like an oak stain is poured. To accompany this, you could purchase a 'sav and a slice'. A string of the former are retrieved from the boiling steamer and one of these tasty smokers are severed from the necklace, a thickish slice of bread spread with Sainsbury's famous Crelos.* If required this also could be smothered with sauce satisfying the evening pangs of hunger. Should we return to the High Street, we will see the piles of litter

---

*Sainsburys Crelos, was their original substitute for butter, and popular in the period.

left as a result of an industrious day, being cleared by the council cleaners, complete with dustcarts. Thanks to these men, the High Street will present a complete change of appearance as a clean and quiet thoroughfare for the following Sunday morning.

CHAPTER 10

The Initial Post

ON leaving school at Christmas 1920, I was quickly sold into slavery. At a social function held by an obscure family friend, I was spotted by a man who saw me as a likely lad to employ. He owned a small credit drapery business and under the guise "he would teach me the trade" succeeded in ensnaring me for this purpose.

This heavily built, mean cruel natured person, could have stepped from the pages of a Dicken's novel with ease with his wispy hair, failing miserably to hide his balding head, and piggy eyes which were not concealed by the gold rimmed small lensed glasses. He had a face that appeared to be flattened from the chin upwards. His sensual lips took on a sneer which was intended to be a smile on the rare occasions he was pleased. A slightly paunchy stomach displayed a heavy gold watch-chain with the insignia attached to denote he was a member of a society to which he was no criterion. This was often handled by his fat hairy hands, with fingers similar to small sausages. The small left finger displayed his late wife's wedding ring, while another large diamond variety flashed on the right. I had not met his first wife, but could not help feeling she must have been happier, wherever she was, than being tied to him. Although this man has long since joined, whoever his type join in after life. Here you have a very conservative description of Mr. Crook in the 20s. I spent nearly three wasted years in his employ before entering the plastering trade and hard as plastering proved to be, it was far more gratifying than the dreary time spent at Crooks.

Mother had journeyed with me to his Victorian sub-basement house in London Fields, with the purpose of negotiating terms for my exploitation. She acquiesced readily to his demands without a murmur, for ten shillings per week with no mention of the hours of service or conditions.

On my arrival the following morning at 9 a.m. I was ushered into the front basement room which served as "the shop". Under the bay window, with the folding shutters, was an ink stained large table, used as a desk and holding among other things, several ledgers and an enormous sales book. This ledger had not been posted for a year. Adjoining was a rude home made counter, with another table on the opposite side. This supported an overmantle, serving as a mirror for the customers who were foolish enough to be persuaded to purchase his coats, which had been in stock for years. Two strips of threadbare carpets on each side of the counter, failed to hide the worn brown lino covered floor. A gas fired radiator, turned low, was the only heating permitted and a single inverted gaslight hung from the centre of this uninspiring room, which was part shop, part office, with every available space holding stock in trade. On entering this dreary sub-basement room, thoughts of Mr. Sowerberry's undertakers shop featured in that famous novel "Oliver Twist" flashed across my mind. The atmosphere and aspect of it in one word was grim! Thank goodness, no coffins were in evidence. There were strings of hob nailed boots, and a dusty sheet covering equally dusty coats, emenating an odour which mingled with the peculiar strong smell from the bales of unbleached calico, that was not exactly conducive to my nostrils.

My first order from him was to "shake the mats, sweep the shop and dust around". Of all the irksome tasks I had been subjected to at home, they were not of this nature.

Considering how I had meticulously prepared myself in anticipation to my venture into business life, this beginning came as a shock and in short humiliating. I hardly anticipated house work, especially so when dressed in my best with carefully brushed hair and highly polished boots. My next task was to cast up the long neglected sales book. This alone gave me a headache, in proportion to the size of the book itself. By 5p.m. I was beginning to long for home, only to be brought a cup of tea and some bread and jam. This was so unexpected, so also was the request to unravel bundles of knotted string and fold up the paper salvaged from the parcels delivered from various warehouses. It was obvious Mr. Crook who had now appeared to light the gas was determined to procure his pound of flesh and sweat from me until 7pm. It had only been two days since I had left school and been free at 4.15 p.m. Remaining in this totally strange environment seemed interminable – and all for one shilling and eight pence per day, less 6d per day fare. It was at that time I was released from bondage and allowed to leave, arriving home at 8.30pm. Such was my initiation into business life.

The Saturday saw me accompanying Mr. Crook on his round collecting from his debtors for goods sold at exorbitant prices. The introduction to the worst slums of Hoxton, Shoreditch and Bethnal Green appalled me in my innocence. Walthamstow had no comparison to the streets and courts we traversed. Lurid tales of crime and murder were recounted during the long distances between clients. The street in which a policeman was murdered and hid in a drain was a highlight of his repertoire. Nile Street, Ware Street, Axe Place, were but a few of the worst type of slums to which I was introduced. Later I had to call alone to collect his dues – I was aged 14! Previously, I had literally limped alongside his giant strides compared with my own clockwork paces.

A block of buildings (now demolished) in one of the many squares was the scene of an incredible happening. At dusk the caretaker of these awful dwellings consisting of one wash-house and one lavatory per landing, serving four flats, would emerge from his ground floor flat armed with a large spanner. In a stentorian voice he would shout "Gas On". This would signal the tenants above to apply a light to the open jet on the landing. This ritual was so common, that all were aware of the warning. If they were not, the smell of gas would soon remind them. The crass stupidity of this occurrence is hardly credible, but so were some of East London's courts and passages in the early 20s. The actual dwellings portrayed in social history books of Victorian times were still in existence, during my initiation into the "The RARND" (the round). This man's vocabulary equalled his looks. It was an affront to the pure Cockney accent.

To end my very brief description of the environment in which I was reluctantly involved there is one disgusting yet apparent commonplace event which sickened me when first witnessed. There were three harridens gossiping outside their hovels in a court now demolished off Bethnal Green Road. As I passed, one of these "ladies" urinated where she stood upright, while carrying on her conversation, to the complete unconcern of her cronies. This impression is imprinted on my mind and its psychological effect took a while before I could reconcile creditable thoughts towards women.

It was not long before two more victims, as myself, were employed and ultimately given adult tasks. Chinese labour was proving profitable, or so Crook thought, until one of these youths proved not too honest a character. He had amorous leanings as well as finding means to supplement his meagre salary. He was also successful in placing his newly found female friend in the family way. Coupled with both problems, he joined H.M. Forces as a boy soldier at age 16, leaving Crook without notice. His intended escape from his commitments were to no avail. On his return from overseas, he was "collared" for maintenance. It was not easy to escape in the 20's.

The second boy employed, John Harvey, was entirely the opposite. He and I became firm friends and remained in touch until his sad demise in 1965. His marriage to a mutual girl friend, was one of the happiest. Time and space will not allow me to recount the experiences and escapades we mutually enjoyed. I reiterate, the time spent at Crooks was hated and wasted years and I prefer to leave them unaccounted.

There is a little known connection with "Crookie" and Walthamstow. A fleet of pirate buses ran through that town and were based at Reliance garage in Chingford, still bearing the name of the original company. The idea and success of the company came from two employees of the London General

Omnibus Co. It was their brains and brawn that helped to enrich Crook, although he initially financed the project.

A final example of this man's character is epitomised by his second wife, who had previously been the "scivvy" of his household. This kindly lady, much younger, presented him with a son very soon after becoming his second wife. On the day after confinement she continued her book-keeping activities in bed! Her spouse could not see her wasting business time! The new son died of diptheria later.

After nearly three wasted years at Crooks, I became aware of the futility of remaining there. In spite of the irregular employment as a plasterer, I decided to throw in my lot, and put myself under the temperamental wing of my father.

CHAPTER 11

Building Trade Period

AS a preface to the above period from 1923-1932, I will endeavour to portray the conditions prevailing at that time. Although bad in many respects, compared with the present day, they were not so very far removed from the Edwardian times. To one interested in this section of social history, I thoroughly recommend Robert Tressals only book "The Ragged Trousers Philanthropists".

It depicts his own experience as a painter in the early part of the century, which gives a very clear picture and is also cynically amusing*.

Hard as my own experiences were, I was not required to "Go on Tramp" in search of employment, although long distances had to be made to secure work.

At the end of the 19th Century my father did however, when necessary, leave home, and walk to wherever a large contract was known to be carried out. On these journeys various con tricks, known as "lays", were performed, the first two mentioned, he was very adept, the third he did not indulge in, although he knew some who carried it out. Life was obviously hard, shouldering responsibilities, and carrying the meagre requirements, plus tools of the trade, on these treks.

Father always travelled with a "Partner". It was on these occasions, when the "Walk Fake Lay" was performed.

On approaching a small town or village one would strip to his undershirt, turn his trousers up as high as possible, turn his hat inside out, and generally create an appearance to draw attention.

The other miscreant would precede and attract a crowd by any means and announce that "Pedro Polinski the famous Russian harrier was walking to ---- relying on voluntary support on the way. This was as a result of a challenge from Lord So and So, who would contribute to charity etc". "He will soon be passing this way! Please assist!"

Enthusiasm would be aroused among the simple minded folk. It must be realised, excitement and events were rare in the village communities.

---

*Regrettably the author died of T.B., the scourge of that period. One cannot be surprised of the various diseases, some connected with the trade, one being Dermatitis, through the unhygienic conditions, prevailing even during my experience as a plasterer. Some of the descriptions portrayed in the ensuing chapter may appear distasteful, nevertheless, they are necessary if one is to envisage a true picture.

Later "Pedro Polinsky" would arrive, striding and sweating and without stopping to acknowledge the cheers, resulting from the previous introduction. A collection would be made by the announcer, and later shared between the two con men.

The second trick required a different approach. A suitable inn would be selected, well crowded, and the tricksters would enter separately in different bars. Both would get into friendly conversation with whoever appeared conducive. Eventually conversation would veer to thought reading and second sight. Father or his partner, whichever had agreed, would pronounce his expertise in this skill, while assuring he could foretell everyones name in the inn. A collection was made, on the understanding it would go to charity – *if he failed*. Names were written on slips, folded and placed in a hat. First one picked and placed, by the thought reader, on his forehead and a name pronounced. "That's mine"! his partner shouts, in feigned surprise. The reader then immediately consults the paper to prove his forecast and places it in his pocket. He can then observe the next name. In this manner, he can continue with the forecast. Favourable circumstances have proved this quite successful. Another lay, which was distasteful, but used generally by vagrants, was known as "The Toke Fake Lay". A lone decrepid con man would seize a previously planted, mouldy lump of bread and devour it hungrily. His brother in crime would bring the pitiful sight to the notice of passers by, and start a collection, with the usual result. Good class neighbourhoods were selected for this swindle. These episodes were passed to me by father when reminiscing on his early days during last century:-

When presenting myself for the first time as a plasterer father was the Foreman working direct for "Coxheads" Builders in Leyton, who were erecting the now "Keswick Hall" in Boundary Road, Walthamstow. This same Chapel has previously been mentioned, in my encounter with the Evangelist.

Father's skill as a teacher in no way compared with his prowess as a plasterer, and with no previous instruction he placed the tools of trade in my hands and told me "to get on with it".

He also had the temerity to request one shilling per hour for my services, having told the builder I was an "experienced improver". My embarrassment and concern, which at times brought me out in cold sweats, was not pleasant, but there it was. I was suddenly thrown in at the deep end and I just had to extricate myself as soon as possible.

Circumstances did not help, when on receiving my first week's wages of £2.10.0, he extracted £1.0.0. for himself on the admission to me that he had had to make up for my shortcomings. Although this may have been correct, it was not exactly conducive to me.

However, I learned quickly and soon had the courage to request my full dues, whereupon he ceased deducting this portion.

The transitional period of being successful in placing the materials on the walls and ceiling, and above all making a good finish, instead of spending a deal of time picking it up off the floor, was now over. I was gaining confidence and experience rapidly. I could by now remove my apron without having first to clear the residue of the used materials from its capacious pocket.

To enter into the variations of plastering would not only be boring to some but would need volumes, but it must be emphasised the forming of mouldings, enrichments, and also making them, in a specialist workshop, could be most interesting and versatile. This section of the trade I experienced when I left father, which occurred approximately nine months later. It happened his disgruntled manner began to pall on me, especially when I was informed by him "I was not worth tuppence a bloody hour". Probably he had lost heavily on his gee gees. Whatever the reason it was on the following morning around 6.30a.m. when we were both preparing to leave home, prior to catching the 2d workmens to the City. I almost tearfully asked "Do you want me to accompany you or not?" to which I received the terse reply "Please your bloody self". This I did by immediately leaving the house to look for employment independently. I had previously always relied on him to secure work.

I was successful in obtaining employment on the rebuilding of the "Clapton Rink Cinema", then sited in Upper Clapton Road, as an improver at 1/6d per hour. My task was to assist a kindly and helpful plasterer on the finer qualities of the trade. I owe much to this gentleman, rejoicing in the name of Jack Long, who sadly suffered from valvular disease of the heart. He in turn was grateful to me as I completed all work which required stooping, an attitude that was not conducive to his complaint.

So my independent career began – I was free from father's idiosyncracies. In the ensuing years I was successful in mastering the arts of the trade, whilst commanding the prolific rate of 2/- per hour, which was in excess of the union rate of 1/9½d. During this period father had aged rapidly and it later fell to me to secure him employment. This was a sad reversal of events. It became embarrassing, not to say difficult, for me to cover up his poorly finished work, owing to his deteriorating eyesight. This was not improved by his habit of purchasing ready made spectacles, sold in Woolworths, at 6d per pair! These small visioned steel rimmed specimens were obviously inferior to the correct eye tested variety. Sometimes, for a change, he would borrow mother's spare pair, with dire results.

After a while we joined forces again, ironically enough, myself being the one to secure work for both, and, in some cases, myself as foreman.

In spite of everything his short lived drinking events occurred, but less frequently. On one occasion he did not return from lunch, having partaken it in the nearest public house. Being Friday it was the day time sheets were completed for wages to be paid on the Saturday. "Under the old pals act" the general foreman, a personal friend of mine, completed father's sheet, allowing him full time for his absence on that Friday afternoon. This, in turn, was submitted to his father that night for wages to be made up for Saturday payment. (Note: the general foreman was the builders son.) Imagine his and my embarrasment, when we were informed by his very irate father (the builder), that George Walker had presented himself on Friday afternoon in an inebriated condition at the builder's office, to collect his wages. Without doubt with the idea of replenishing his cash, in order to continue his boozing in the early evening.

Naturally, both the foreman and myself lost prestige and trust in the eyes of Mr. Darby senior, for falsifying the time sheets (and rightly so). But what did father care? I shall never know.

His irresponsible acts at times could be infuriating, although his general good character outweighed these. One other episode which now appears amusing, was not so at the time. We were being employed by The Bethnal Green Board of Guardians, at their childrens home, opposite "The Green Man", Leytonstone. The contrast in this employment, as opposed to contract builders, was very favourable. With the conducive surroundings, one could use the word "easy".

To clarify the term "easy" infers one was not being continually harassed by the worried foreman, saying "Hurry up" or "The job's in debt, if you can't move faster, I'll have to get someone who can." A host of similar frightening phrases were used, purporting that your employment was in jeopardy, and that plenty of tradesmen were available to replace you. The absence of these innuendos created a far more pleasant atmosphere, and consequently was appreciated.

Father and I were the only "spreads"* (i.e. plasterers) on this site. Following his usual trek to "The Green Man" at lunch time, he returned with a well quenched thirst and a lethargic feeling which without doubt was enhanced by the heat of the beautiful summer day. In his befuddled state

---

*Trade name for Plasterer, (Carpenter: Chippy) (Electrician: Sparks) (Painter: Skip) (Steel Erector: Iron Fighter). A fortunate regular employee known as "A Royal".

rather than take up his hawk and trowel, he thought it a better idea to crawl beneath a large and wonderful Weeping Willow tree whose tresses swept the ground. Here he fell into the arms of Morpheus with a seraphic smile on his face whilst being completely concealed. It is necessary to add this children's home was set in extensive grounds with a considerable number of trees and shrubs. I would love to have followed suit, but as a loyal and dutiful son, I doubled my efforts at work with an endeavour to cover up his absence, also hoping that the general foreman would keep out of the way.

The newly built bathrooms on which we were working were on the ground floor, so I could keep an eye open to any approach across the lawns. All went well until about 4 p.m. when Bill, the general foreman, appeared on the horizon. He was entirely out of character for the type of job he had.

A benign and kindly soul, having also spent many years as a council maintenance worker, he had obviously enjoyed what was commonly known as "a soft number" never having to qualify a day's work, or worry whether the contract paid or not.

It was most fortunate for father again that Bill the foreman was of this type. He espied father on his back, snoring away and oblivious of all his surroundings, whilst polluting the atmosphere with Mann & Crossmans fumes of strong ale. He shook him to wakefulness exclaiming "George! I'm surprised at you!" I thought "I'm bloody well not!" In fact I would have been surprised at not being surprised at any escapade that father was involved.

Once again the incident passed with forgiveness by the foreman, providing it did not happen again. Such was his leniency and a full day's pay was received which compensated father – but not myself who had slogged and sweated with both work and trepidation during that afternoon.

His outlook was the exact opposite of my own and was oblivious to any worry or future aspirations. In fact to live for today and to hell with the future was the general outlook of the majority of building operatives in those days. Such an example is typified in one of father's cronies "Charlie Bradds" or better known as "Snowy", a Walthamstow character supreme.

A priceless photo of him is shown in this book. The nickname "Snowy" was obviously taken from his albino white hair. He was a born comedian, standing 5' nothing and often referred to locally as "Charlie Chaplin". His escapades were many. When off duty, he dressed in a dashing style with a carnation or similar buttonhole. When travelling on bus, train or tram car, he invariably placed his ticket in his eye as a monocle, and affected a high pitched frosty voice. With this exaggerated top draw accent he drew laughter spontaneously from the fellow passengers.

If ever father was late home from work, mother's immediate reaction was

Snowey Bradds with a sample of his handiwork: note tram ticket in eye.

"He is with that bloody Snowy again". Poor Snowy! It's amazing how innocent parties are blamed rather than the ones who are the real culprits, by allowing themselves to be persuaded.

While employed on a country project, he approached the unsuspecting landlady of the village inn. During a pleasant conversation, while regaling himself with her brew of ale, he endeared himself to her, and gained complete confidence. (He had a most engaging manner with women). Following his inference that he was the foreman on job in the vicinity, he made the following suggestion, "My dear madam, I am forever putting my hand in my bleeding pocket at the continued requests from my men for 'subs'*. I would be most obliged if you could open an account for them, and I will settle the score† on Saturday". To this eloquent appeal in his top draw voice the dear madam agreed. Consequently on the day of reckoning he sought payment from the dozen or so workmen, who in turn appeared to have poor memories regarding amount of liquid refreshment they had consumed. However, their meagre contribution was collected by Snowy who repaired to the expectant lady and, in his most superior voice, asked, "What is the score madam?" To which she quoted the required amount. Snowy then quite honestly placed the whole of his collection on the counter which proved quite insufficient. In a surprised tone he remarked, "You must be mistaken madam, this amount is what my men have given me, and that's all you can have." "Then I shall sue you," said the dear madam. Snowy, never at a loss, rejoined "And I shall sue you, too, for enticing my men to get drunk". Finally the farce was reconciled, but the episode gives an example of his rare character.

Another occasion when repairing council houses which had sustained bomb damage, but were still being occupied, he was found by the lady of the house, blithely asleep in her bed, fully clothed. It leaves little imagination to envisage her reaction, followed by his hasty retreat. It was without doubt actuated by the warm weather, mid-day beer and heavy lunch, not withstanding his guile.

In direct opposite I cite Jack Thorne, a tall angular strictly abstemious person with a thin cadaverous face adorned by a wispy drooping moustache and very bright pale blue eyes. He always wore a shabby overcoat, winter or summer. He considered himself thrifty, others thought him "bloody mean". He excelled as a plasterer, and was the proud possessor of his own house in Coppermill Lane, E.17. This was an extremely rare achievement and practically unheard of in the era of 1912.

---

*Subbing – Lending
†Score – Amount

He was disliked by many who were jealous of his little Empire, and he often called at our house at the time he knew father would be having his tea. His reason being "Did father know of a job?". Also, he was sure of a cup of tea, and possibly a piece of mother's heavy bread pudding. The spectre of unemployment was always present, and the unfortunate relied on the fortunate, to assist each other in this endless quest.

Mother, father and myself were once invited to his home for a Sunday tea. Mrs. Thorne had to be seen to be believed. A heavy jowled dark woman with pendulous lips, sagging bags below the jet black eyes, a large mole sprouting beneath her lower lip which helped to detract your attention from the rest of her body, which was of ample proportions. Added to all this, she was slightly deaf, and had a throaty bass loud voice. I can never remember her being dressed in anything but black, including a bonnet of that period. It would not be unkind to the old Queen Victoria, to say that Mrs Thorne could have passed easily as a stand-in for that Royal person. She entertained us later by accompanying herself on the piano, in a doleful heart-rendering fashion. Whenever in her company, we were subjected to this "treat". Her favourite number was "I am but a poor blind boy", whilst Jack pulled faces behind her back, to my intense amusement.

I liked him as a kid, to me he was fun. This entertainment followed tea, which in itself nearly caused mother to have apoplexy. In preparation for tea, the rarely used best cups were removed from the dresser, and moistened by Mrs Thorne's breath before being polished with a well used tea towel. Much the same method is used when polishing spectacles. Our dear Jack, emerged from the scullery, carrying a loaf of bread on his head, winkles and watercress on one plate, and a pot of "Pinks" jam*, in either hand. Having endured the tea, we were induced into the front room, leaving the residue of the feast to the flies. An impromptu soirée followed with Bertha Thorne performing on the pianoforte to her bass voice. Her favourite song was as repetitive as the pop songs of to-day –

It was as follows:
I am but a poor blind boy
Though my heart is full of joy
When I lay me down to rest
By my saviour I am blessed
Chorus
They love me,
Yes they love me

---

*Pinks Jam was cheap product, that even mother refused to buy.

And to me they are all kind,
They love me
Yes they love me
Oh they love me
Because I'm blind.

He must have been the most conceited of all the blind boys known. He was so sure everybody loved him.

Jack was a great favourite of mine, having no children of his own he took delight in entertaining me and excelled as a ventriloquist. His favourite performance was speaking to an imaginary person up the chimney and throwing his voice in reply. Although he was extremely mean and was not known to part with a penny, his love of children was obvious to me, and appreciated. Later in life, I had the pleasure of working with poor old Jack and although he was considerably older, was just as amusing – and still wore his overcoat.

Being an exponent of private enterprise my friend and I hit upon a plan to possibly increase our limited income. It was on a certain and most prominent building being erected in London, adjacent to the Embankment, that my partner, both in work and crime, decided we would run "A Crown and Anchor" board, during the dinner hour of 12noon–1pm. Having seen others run this age old game of chance, and as gambling was rife on this particular job, why not us? We had experienced how easy it was to lose on this gamble as punters. Careful preparations were made, and in due course, we set up our position on the top floor. Little did we realise how fortunate we were in picking the top floor, although actually the top floor picked us, as we were working there at the time. It was so successful. Play started as the last notes of the dinner whistle faded. Sandwiches were scoffed while bets were being considered and nishes* were made.

It was amazing how many persons were anxious to lose their money as quickly as possible. At times my partner and I were sometimes concerned about our well-being, when a burly navvy – or any other tradesman of uncertain temperament – lost a fair amount of money and on some occasions demanded credit. We were also concerned when the foreman joined in, in case he lost!

However, it so happened much gambling was going on in this edifice, including bookies touts, who regularly collected betting slips, and distributed football lists known then as short and long lists, which required the punter to

---

*"Nish" slang word meaning to toss a coin in deciding which square to bet on.

forecast matches at fixed odds. My one achievement was predicting 4 aways, thus winning the terrific amount of £4, and was immediately asked by all and sundry "Was I going to have a party"?

In consequence of the publicity, the police became aware of a miniature Monte Carlo in their midst and decided to stage a raid on the premises. No-one was aware of this until plain-clothes men in rough working suits appeared from nowhere and proceeded to make arrests. The chaos was extremely amusing to those not involved. Miscreants went to any length to divest themselves of any incriminating evidence. Card players grabbed up loose change, innocent expressions displayed – betting slips hidden anywhere near at hand, while our crown and anchor board was thrown out of the window, before the arm of the law reached our department of "The Casino". It appeared the main persons required by the police were the street corner bookie and his runners, who were trapped well and truly. Although a few workmen were fined for running a similar sort of game as ourselves, it passed off leaving gossip for weeks, and a sudden reformation towards gambling of any description. We abandoned our venture and failed to recover our nerve, or our board. We did, however, retain the dice after wading about in a water tank in which they were dropped. I doubt whether such an event has ever happened before or since, and certainly will not in the future, for the simple reason of changes in the law, and conditions. The new method and mechanisation seem to have created a new type of workmen. This remark poses a question, left to debate, while I keep my own counsel.

Accommodation for meals were, in some instances, non-existent or inadequate. At the very blast of the whistle by the timekeeper, whose other main tool of trade consisted of a large gunmetal watch which was above reproach as a perfect chronometer, and caused everyone to drop tools and seek a clear spot to replenish the inner man.

Some of the old hands used the nearest pub, while the majority dusted the floor with their cap, placed a plank of wood against the wall for a back rest, and sat on the spot previously cleared of debris. It was in this primitive manner they had to partake of whatever had been packed. There was in some cases a small hut known as the "Mess Room" where a witches brew was made and referred to as tea! This liquid took on a mahogany hue and was manufactured in a galvanised iron bucket, which was blackened by soot on the outside and heavily stained by tannin on the inside. On the top of this swirling liquid, floated a piece of wood, also stained, which was reputed to eliminate the smokey taste caused by the open fire on which it boiled merrily.

The tea boy, that invaluable employee, was dogsbody to all and sundry, and in his spare time did a bit of labouring. He would pierce a full condensed milk tin in two places, by hammer and nail, then proceeded to place his mouth to one hole, blowing as hard as possible, and so evict the contents to complete the ultimate and final product.

He would have all the enamel mugs to hand, which had been dipped in the water tank for cleaning. The tank was also used for washing tools and all building purposes. The mugs were now fully-prepared to be again immersed in the swirling mass for the lucky owners who had paid each week. for the service rendered.

Whatever this poor runabout charged for his secret recipe, it made no difference to us all. "He was making a fortune out of his private enterprise," was our unanimous opinion.

I often wondered what happened to any escaping saliva whilst he was executing the blowing act. If it did enter the tin, it was of no consequence, as he reserved the tin for his own drinking vessel and thus had the maximum share of condensed milk.

The plumbers shop was also a popular venue for meals. The smell of tallow, lead and paraffin added to the enchantment. Holding a sandwich in one hand and manipulating playing cards in the other was a skilful procedure as a school of gamblers were always in attendance.

The most notorious "Mess Room" I ever encountered was on the site when "Unilever House", Blackfriars, was being erected about 1930. It was situated in the sub basement, with exposed open drains, debris and sundry building materials littered the area. A long bench made up of scaffold boards acted as a dining table, whilst the most comfortable seat comprised of a sack, partly filled with wood shavings and placed on an empty drum. Alternatively a wheelbarrow tipped forward on its shafts, can be quite comfortable. Try it some time! A wooden barrow is best. It was not surprising, therefore, on this particular job, I chose to speculate a shilling on an egg and chips in a cafe directly opposite the job. Although this became rather difficult, as in winter we were confined to half hour for lunch or dinner. If one was working on the top floors, by the time the ladders were climbed, and the busy city street negotiated, one was lucky not to finish up with a severe bout of indigestion. Bad as eating arrangements were, the attention to latrines by the contractors were positively abysmal.

It was on this job I won a dubious bottle of port in the Christmas raffle. My brother and I greedily consumed this on the Friday evening before Christmas Eve, in company with a large supper of fried fish and chips.

In the early hours, my unpredictable digestive system gave warning that it objected to this unusual intrusion. Feeling far from well, I bravely rose at 6 a.m. and journeyed as usual to work.

Mann Crossmans Sports Pavillion in construction, Billet Road, E17. Approx. 1927. The author (cap in hand middle row) as a plasterer.

About 10 a.m., after the tea-boy had delivered his brew, my stomach decided to eliminate some of its disturbing contents. To my partner, Ernie Renny, also from Walthamstow, I was becoming a liability. It was very fortunate there were no workmen below us.

Eventually, I had to inform the foreman, to whom we had a friendly rapport, that "I will have to pack up Fred". His genuine disappointment was obvious and, in an appealing reply, said, "hang on until 12 o'clock, I've arranged a piss up".

I failed to be attracted. The thought of this was horrific.

The next scene saw me hanging on the hand rail on the platform of a General Bus, distributing the residue of my previous night's orgy. being Christmas Eve, it was not an unusual sight to see a person in disgrace, as myself, although rarely on the rear end of a bus.

On many contracts, even those in London, the lavatories consisted of a long deep trench, with a wooden pole placed on supports. This primitive arrangement was enclosed by a ramshackle shed open at each end. This unhygienic contraption could accommodate quite a number of customers. It does not require a great deal of imagination to envisage the sight of five or six men sitting side by side reading a page of newspaper, to be utilised later for the obvious purpose, also the added effluvier arising from the results of their concerted efforts. At times buckets were placed in out of the way places for use as a urinal. These were seldom emptied, so there was no need to look for these receptacles, one only had to use his sense of smell.

Of course, if buckets were provided or not, various corners were used, as was inevitable. The opportunity of washing your hands was the usual water tank, available on all floors, with the use of your apron for a substitute towel.

There were many old chestnuts handed down, concerning the building trades. One in particular portrayed a navvy, who had accidentally allowed his coat to fall in the cess pit, and was endeavouring to recover same with a larry*. His friend exclaimed "You won't be able to wear it Fred". To which Fred replied "It's not the coat I'm worrying about, it's my dinner in the pocket". Although this crude humour appears in bad taste, it was typical and, compared with the sick humour and pornograhic viewing of today, it is quite innocuous. The trade unions strength was weakened as the demand for tradesmen lessened. The one to which I belonged rejoiced by the multifarious title of "The National Amalgamated Trade Union of Plasterers Granolithic and Cement Workers". Father, having joined lapsed and then rejoined,

---

*Larry – A now obsolete tool comprising of a long handle with an open steel blade at the end, which was used for mixing lime hair and sand, known as coarse stuff.

finally became a member at the Hagerston branch which, as usual, met in the club room of a pub.

At first I enjoyed the trek to pay subs on periodic Saturday evenings. The amble along "The Kingsland Waste", an open market closely akin to our High Street, offered a specialist attraction. Its predominance in gramophone, musical and photographic stalls, with a new and exciting introduction of crystal sets was unique. The strains of jazz bands and stentorian vocalists, emanating from the large horn phonographs were wonderful. "Ukelele Lady" "Because I Love You" "All Alone" – maudlin ballads, mixed with hot jazz, filled the air.

This Saturday evening task soon became irksome, as more interesting pastimes became apparent. Motorcycling and the charming "Flappers of the 20s" were far more conducive than the solitary journeys to pay Union dues in the formal environment of an East End pub.

A sleek Rudge Whitworth, with a bobbed-haired, short-skirted companion, had a far greater attraction and it was to this status I was now able to achieve. The skirts of these modern girls became even shorter when the vivacious females perched themselves delicately on the pillion seat. It was a classical pose, not to say delight, in observing a trim figure with arched back and fulsome front pressed affectionately against the back of her knight in shining leather coat, even if the coat was on H.P. as also the cycle.

Ample proportions of her legs would be exposed by the cunningly arranged high foot rests. This may have appeared indecorous to some, but certainly not to the motorist following at the rear.

Competition was rife by both sexes for a unique partner. The male would be looking for a companion who could ride with expertise and sway with the cornering at the right angle, rather than the wary, who would wobble and clutch him with fear, as opposed to affection, and in so doing be a menace to both.

The female, on the other hand, would be casting an eye on the comfort of the pillion, plus the prestige of the rider.

A high regard was shown to members of the Walthamstow Motor Club. For one thing, they could all be identified by the badge affixed to the rear of their steed.

Before leaving this interesting interlude, I would like to mention one young lady named "Thora", who was the "Champion Leg Exposer" of the era. Maybe some will still remember this delightful companion. Alternatively, Nobby Freshwater who possessed the hardest brick-like pillion of all times. It was unfortunate for anyone who were beguiled to accept his offer "for a ride", both male or female, they could be assured of a bruised bottom for weeks. Speculation in purchasing an air cushion always paid dividends.

However, as a result of my newly-acquired interest, I transferred to Lodge No. 12 held at "The Standard", Blackhorse Lane, where I was among many I knew and had worked with. The atmosphere was far more convivial while the meetings were held on Fridays.

Among the fraternity of plasterers was one "Harry Parkes" who, although belligerent when drunk, was quite friendly when sober. He was a wiry, rather rodent faced person, whose front teeth had allegedly been lost in a fracas, originating in a public house urinal. This did not enhance his appearance, which was in some way reminiscent of a junior Dracula, his side fangs standing out conspicuously when laughing – or sneering. The fact he was slightly crippled, owing to being wounded in the 1914–18 War, evoked sympathy when his pain was evident. He took great pride in proposing me as auditor to the branch, as I was an "edicated young man". This proposition was seconded and passed, before I had a chance to accept or refuse. The chairman will forever be remembered (by those fortunate enough) for his famous and regular call to order. This reprimand in a rich cockney nasal voice "Order, please, there are too many 'arf pints being drunk at the meeting and before"! I quite realised his difficult task of conducting the meeting, whilst malefactors wandered up and down the stairs, carrying their glasses of beer. The loud buzz of conversation and the clattering of boots on the iron staircase, intermingled with raucous laughter, was in no way conducive to the serious business being discussed among the respective Brothers. It was a night of escape, anyway, from the slog of the day.

Whilst one was employed, the dreaded threat of the sack always hung over everyone. The cry "The jobs in debt. You will have to move quicker" were commonplace phrases. It always surprised me that a contract ever resulted in a profit in view of the foreman's menacing observations. Termination of the contract invariably saw the arrival of the foreman with National Health and Unemployment Cards (coloquially known as "Map Book and Guide") The sense of humour prevailed, even if the spirits were low. The philosophical attitude remained. The notice of one hour was given, in which time tools were cleaned and packed, aprons or overalls folded, with the thoughts of where to look for work on the morrow.

During the miniature boom, when Regent Street was being rebuilt in the 20's plus erection of super cinemas, the spectre of unemployment receded, but the conditions remained the same.

After I had been successful in obtaining work, by traipsing London enquiring "Do you need a spread?" (plasterer) I would remain in the metropolis and celebrate with a 6d seat in the gallery of a theatre. Any thriller running was my absolute favourite – "The Ghost Train", "The Ringer", "The Terror" were but a few that kept me enthralled. Seated in a cramped position, with a perpendicular view of the stage, which appeared as if you were looking through the wrong end of a telescope, did not deter my enthusiasm for this treat.

The green plush seats of "Wyndams" and the pink one of "The Garrick" that furnished the stalls of those two famous theatres, made me determined I would one day be seated in one.

The desire to improve my position brought thoughts of emigration to the U.S.A. The fact that plasterers were in demand and high rewards obtained, influenced me to contact our friends, the Adams, of Boundary Road, who had emigrated years earlier. Following a protracted spate of correspondence, a mutual arrangement had been made to temporarily stay with the Adam family in Chicago. On the 23rd October, 1929, the Wall Street Crash came to a climax and the following day became known in history as Black Thursday. One of the worst financial crises known had reached its peak and the slide continued until 1932. People's savings were wiped out overnight, such was the culmination of speculating without discretion, and the skulduggery of others. Suicides were occurring owing to ruination of many. The country was in a parlous state! To proceed with my project would have been foolish, especially as my friends were also victims. So I close this chapter, that but for this momentous happening in American history, who knows?

Builders outing, Southend Road, 1924. Father ×, myself ○.

CHAPTER 12

The Halls of Pleasure

AT THE age of sixteen, I fell completely in love, as one does at that age, being assured that life forever would be bliss. She was a petite curly-haired pretty blonde, blessed with a good sense of humour, a happy family with a prince among fathers, to whom I had a great admiration. It was through the persuasion of Mary Allen, that being her name, plus my desire to conquer the art of ballroom dancing, that we decided to attend the learners' night at the Workmen's Hall.

The hall still exists in the High Street, sandwiched between two shops opposite the Salvation Army Citadel. In those days one of the shops was "Bunyans" the bookshop, which I haunted for back numbered, dog eared copies of Magnet, Gem, Sexton Blake and hosts of other thrilling weekly boys magazines. I owe my liking for Latin and Greek phrases, which "Mr. Quelch" the Remove Form Master of Greyfriars endeavoured to drive into the skull of Billy Bunter, and at the same time trying to control his recalcitrant pupils. I highly rated the late Frank Richards, author of these yarns, especially for the moral standards he set for his readers.

Having entered the dimly gaslit passage I was eventually lured into the Workmen's Hall on a particular Friday night and introduced to "Dave Wilson".

He was the "Major Domo", ably assisted by a moon faced young man who had a prematurely wrinkled appearance, but possessed amazing agility and expertise in all forms of ballroom dancing. Owing to his unbounding energy and countenance, he was cruelly dubbed by the heartless females as "Monkey". Dave Wilson, the senior instructor, was a small lithesome person aged about 45, thin faced, topped with sparse mousey hair. He always arrived immaculately attired, plus a trilby hat and overcoat. His feet were also permanently encased in dancing pumps while a wing collar and bow completed his tools of trade. On special non-teaching nights, he sported evening dress while his sister "Connie Wilson" provided the band, otherwise a piano sufficed.

The well experienced females were uniformly bedecked in white blouses and ties, all shod in red charleston sandals – in order to be "with it". The more affluent proudly displayed short fringe skirts, disclosing plenty of leg above the knee, as it swung to and fro, some more shapely than others. These skirts did enable freedom of movement required by "the Charleston" and "Black Bottom".

The hall itself was a cold looking affair, equally living up to its name. The very first thing that impressed me, both physically and mentally, was the heavily knotted wooden block floor, not the usual smooth blocks, but those of a larger soft wood type and used profusely in school rooms. The same well-worn blocks graced the floors of Gamuel Road School. They wore so unevenly that the many knots stood up like miniature molehills. In general, one's boots or shoes were worn to very thin proportions, consequently the knots impressed themselves into the thin soles and eventually the ball of one's foot. The effect was painful enough walking, let alone dancing.

Credit is due to Dave, who expertly demonstrated the dances while being partnered by one of the clique of the "regular" flappers. These "experts" always congregated as an elite bunch, beneath Connie Wilsons Band (sister to Dave) which graced the tiny stage. It was amusing to see these sophisticated birds of the 20s vie with each other to catch the beckoning eye of their own Valentino, thus giving them the opportunity to sweep into the glancing slide of a tango, or alternatively, the high ebullient jig of the Charleston. Whatever the demonstration was, it required more skill than of today's counterpart, when one appears to be suffering from the shakes while endeavouring to dislocate their neck.

On special nights, the band would be enhanced by "Wally Buck", the Coppermill Lane tonsorial artiste, whose prowess with the newly recognised saxophone was superb. After many attempts I was able to "get around", but it was a long period before I had the temerity to approach an unknown female with the apologetic request for a dance. The hard-boiled Hannahs could be cruel in their sneering rebuffs in refusing to partner, while alternatively there were more females who were as anxious as oneself to improve their skill. In general, a social evening was assured.

Rarely were there any unpleasant happenings excepting on an occasion when two, not too ladylike females, decided to settle a dispute regarding the rights of possession of a particular "Don Juan". One objected to having spearmint pressed in her hair and retaliated by pulling her rival's tresses. Result, stern ejection and permanently barred. Nevertheless, the Workmen's Hall served the same purpose as the Drill Hall. It provided relaxation and pure entertainment for the class who desired that particular pastime.

Apart from the sporting celebrities there were several talented entertainers of repute, two of which I had personal acquaintance, namely Jenny Howard, whose real name was Daisy Blowes, and Arthur Dongray. He appeared under the apt stage name of "Don Gray". Jenny oft times performed at Walthamstow Palace, supported by a host of fans including myself and her cousin, Evelyn Kirkby. We were all members of the Walthamstow and

District Motor Club and great friends. Myself, Frank Haselden, and a few, started the club, which I hope to portray in the future.

Both were great troupers! One of Jenny's hit songs, in which she characterised a saucy Parisien to perfection is worth noting:

I love zee English
Zee English zay love me
Zay seem to like my personality:
Chorus
I got zee eye
Zat make zee wink
Zee wink zat make
Zee fellow zink
I got zee mouse
Zat go like ziss
Oo la la, I am French
And a Frenchie gal can kiss
I got zee style
I got zee smile
Zat make zee old men young la la
Just like a ship rolls on zer sea
Sailors roly poly me
Oo la la, com ce com ca

While Arthur excelled as a pianist, baritone and yodeller, his songs "I'm Tony the Swiss Mountaineer" and others were superb. Both these talented artists first appeared at the municipal concerts held at the High Street Baths, at which the famous pianist, Mark Hambourg, also entertained. The Baths, since demolished, was the most important centre of hygiene*. It catered for the much needed slipper baths, plus swimming facilities in the summer. It is interesting to note entrance fees for swimming was governed by "Clean Days" and "Dirty Days". To elaborate, water was changed Sundays and Wednesdays. Thus on Sunday and Wednesday, the cost was higher, a little less the following days and by Saturday the water took on a murky appearance and was not too inviting to the very particular. It was in some ways reminiscent to a village duck pond. Well, it was only 2d entrance fee with no charge for the extra chlorine!

---

*The nearest facilities for swimming, was an open air pool near the Hollow Ponds at Whipps X. This crude lido was renovated in 1926. I had the distinction of assisting as a plasterer by laying the granite surround. The pool was recently closed.

However the slipper baths were a godsend to many who were unfortunate enough to lack a bathroom which, in itself, was a rare luxury to many householders. I was puzzled by the sign "slipper baths" 1st Class 6d., 2nd Class 2d. Yes, class distinction had even penetrated that field. I often gazed with interest at the huge boilers on view from the side door, and the workmen appearing from the steamy atmosphere. The smell was reminiscent of wash day at home, only more so.

It was not long before I realised I was becoming a trifle too big for the tin bath placed in the scullery, with human traffic in and out like Piccadilly Circus. I was becoming rather conscious of my sex, which caused me to insist on 2d for a venture to the mysterious slipper bath. This bold request came at last after "Murfetts" coalman burst into the scullery with 2cwt of coal on his back and proceeded to shoot the same into the coal cupboard, the gas stove placed in such a position to limit the opening of the door, making it difficult for the frantic coalman to deliver his goods. I received a good shower of black dust which, in any case, acted as a substitute for talcum powder, not that such a luxury was ever foreseeable. I was only aware of "Fullers Earth" as a toilet requisite. It is hardly believable that the coalman had by force of circumstances carried a two hundredweight sack of coals through the passage, now termed "The Hall", mother having previously taken down the lace curtains that adorned the centre. These were just a Victorian embellishment and constituted a nuisance. Mother's constant request to "mind the curtains", was similarly treated as "the boy who cried wolf". An awkward right turn took him through the kitchen, thence to the scullery, when an about turn was performed in order to shoot the black dusty diamonds. The noise and confusion was appalling. When I was very young it had frightening effects on me, causing a flight in terror behind my mother's apron.

The second class bath was quite an experience, the powers that be who designed this ablution did not allow one to arrange his own dispensation of water. This most important requirement was controlled by the massive attendant. (Why were all attendants in those days so Herculian?) His robust body was protected by a rubber apron, his round face and protruding eyes remind me now of Peter Lohre, the film actor, although Peter did not sport the walrus moustache which adorned this gentleman countenance. His whole appearance was befitting a slaughterhouse man, especially enhanced by the large spanner with which he turned on the water from the outside of the bathroom. This could have easily been used to fell an ox. The water simply gushed in from an equally massive pipe like a roaring cataract. When filled to the required height, he promptly cleared off leaving the hapless bather to test the water himself. It was invariably either scalding hot, luke warm or freezing cold. Consequently, then one had to shout "more hot no. 6" or, alternatively, "more cold", whereon others would take up the cry for their requirements. Thus the harassed attendant would join in the shouting match with "wait a bloody minute" or "one at a bleeding time" or some sort of equivalent observation, in his most polite manner.

Supplied with a minute towel which appeared to be made of a dark grey hessian, similar to a coarse apron, was almost useless for its purpose. With only this it was impossible to wipe oneself completely dry, but the tropical atmosphere very soon dried the water on the body only to be replaced by extreme perspiration.

Eventually, when older and earning, I added to the excitement of a weekly bath by rising to the heights of a first class! For this the exact same procedure regarding ration of water was performed, but one was provided with an extra towel of better quality and larger area, also a seat in the bathroom and, wonder of wonders, one piece of yellow soap. It had one other added attraction. There were usually fewer waiting patrons, giving one the superior enactment of "going straight in". To arrive with a spare towel of your own marked you down as a "second classer". "Snobbery in the bath house" sounds like a title for a thriller. The demolition of these character buildings in the metropolis is less a crime than the eyesores erected in their place.

The criminals of the 20s and 30s in Walthamstow were pygmies in comparison with the thugs of to-day. To mention some well-known names is not necessary, although with all their misdemeanours they still had a certain respect for the ethics of "Villaindom".

My friend Walter Chandler who had a most engaging personality, was employed as a salesman at Lambs (motor factors) then in Selbourne Road. He eventually became a director of that firm and, in the course of his position, had transactions with many High Street businessmen. It was through this connection he learned of various escapades in the course of general conversation.

My first recollection of Lambs was of their initial shop, a few doors from "The Chequers", High Street. As a schoolboy I often gazed with envy at the sparkling cycles, costing £4.17.6 each, with a hopeless yearning to possess one. Incidently, at the age of 14 I cashed my one and only war saving certificate and secured a massive 28 inch frame, second-hand Chater-Lea cycle. This model was fitted with one front brake, and should have rightly been displayed in a museum. I will draw a veil over the scene with mother, when admonishing me for "wasting my money".

My ambition later to secure the centre of attraction in that window, was the round tank lightweight Triumph Motorcycle. This was not realised until many years later. Again it was a second-hand B.S.A. which, even at the age of 20, I still received the maternal reprimand albeit with slightly less authority.

Returning to my opening remarks, two of the petty criminals had decided "to *do* Lidstones", then a large emporium at the lower end of High Street, cornering on Pretoria Ave*, where a rear passage exited into the latter thoroughfare. In keeping with their intended secret planning, it might as well have been broadcast on the then one and only channel 2LO. Quite possibly the Walthamstow, Leyton and Chingford Guardian had set their headlines in readiness for the next edition. Such was the secrecy and organising ability on these matters of crime.

On a brilliant moonlight night, entrance was gained at the rear of the premises, prior to a costermongers barrow being parked in Pretoria Avenue. All these elaborate preparations were clearly observed by the eyes of the law concealed in front gardens, and surrounding likely places. The police had obviously prior information of the premeditated crime. No one was more surprised than Bloxey, when he jumped over the wall into the welcoming arms of a stolid English Bobby.

The culprit had unknowingly passed the bales of stolen cloth over the wall to Robert. Bloxey was then ordered to load up his barrow and, with seething indignation, pushed the vehicle not to the "fence", but to the police station. There he had the pleasure of being lodged in the cell next door to his despairing accomplice. Being well and truly nicked, they ruefully admitted it "a fair cop".

At the lower end of Church Hill once stood a white building known as the Drill Hall, for the use of the 7th Essex Territorial Regiment. My good friend Frank Haselden was a keen Territorial and bandsman, and although I shared many adventures with him, I did not have his desire for military diversion. At parties Frank excelled in sporadic accompaniment with the piano, with his "Pyooker", being his interpretation of the trumpet. It added to the fun, excepting when he partly extinguished the fire, when clearing the innards of his instrument of the surplus spittle.

It was at the Drill Hall that boxing bouts were often promoted. Although not on par with the Albert Hall, it did remarkably well sponsoring professional as well as amateur events. In contrast dances were also held, although the surface was hardly fit for ballroom expertise, considering the heavy iron shod army boots that had pounded it for years. To be fair it was slightly worse than the Workmen's Hall.

---

*It was in Pretoria Avenue Mr Simmond invented, produced and exported the famous Pretoria Fire Escapes.

The Drill Hall has, like many structures, suffered demolition and been replaced by buildings which will never recapture the atmosphere or exhibit such sport and entertainment experienced by many. The motley crowd of patrons from urchins, to the elite, and some not so elite were always evident. Many who could not afford ringside seats had to be content with the rear seats, consisting of wooden forms. It was not long during the evening bouts before excitement resulted in standing instead of sitting on the seating arrangement. This procedure often proved fatal when excitement rose to fever pitch and the form would topple over, amid a melee of arms and legs. This resulted in the attendants asserting their authority, which became such monotonous regularity that nobody took any notice.

Among the amateur contestants there was one who was outstanding as well as very popular with all. He was "Stanley Rollings" who, at the time of writing, is still in business in Walthamstow and living in Chingford. Although semi-retired from his long established cabinet making business, at the age of 68, he still reflects his athletic prowess. A modest and rather shy person, being loathe to discuss his victories, especially while he was boxing for his regiment, when on active service in UK, Italy and North Africa. He returned from the world conflict unscathed.

There were, of course, entertaining fighters, armed with more cunning than skill. One in particular, who we will call George, was notorious in originating the most unorthodox style of fighting I had ever witnessed. He would stamp both feet, and simultaneously make a complete body turn, swinging his extended arm very swiftly, sometimes catching his opponent an unexpected smash in the face with the back of his glove.

This action proved to be devastating in some cases, and would have by no means been permitted to-day. But it was *not* today, neither was it the "Albert Hall", and the referee sat in a ringside seat, with complete aplomb. His placidity could have been induced by a previous tonic or two enjoyed in "The Chequers", High Street, which would produce a benign attitude to all and sundry. I have just realised how often the mention of "The Chequers" appears in my reminiscences. It was quite a landmark in this street of events. It happened George did meet a more wily opponent, who meted out a severe battering. It has been reported that the recipient was wandering around later in the evening, his head swathed in bandages, plaintively bemoaning the fact "I can't see". Nemesis had struck!

A more notable and refined bout was between Pat Tarling and Jack Stanley, in which "Pat" won in the first round, and went on to greater heights. He met the Italian man mountain "Carnera" and managed to go four rounds with the "Ambling ape" as he was then known. Quite an achievement!

Stanley Rollings, aged 22, light-heavyweight amateur boxer.

For the benefit of those who remember those halcyon days I mention just a few of the heroes – Reg Pullen, Ruben Dicker, Mick O'Brien, and George Mortenson who, with many more, entertained and thrilled followers of the Drill Hall. The amateurs, such as Stan Rollings, boxed for the sheer love of the sport. As for the professionals who, for the magnificent purses that were offered – e.g. top fight £2.10.0d, lower down the scale 7/6d – it can only be concluded they must have been in urgent need of the money, or alternatively enjoyed a battering, for batterings sake. So obviously no contestant needed a bodyguard to protect him against the possibility of being robbed of his hard-earned reward, although mugging then was an unknown word.

Now on my occasional visits to High Street, I feel saddened at the absence of those landmarks that had served the public for years.

The old Monoux School became a T.B. clinic in the evenings, which at one time I entered with the unholy dread of what my examination would disclose, having been suspect. My fears were eventually allayed. The Conway Hall Congregational Church can no longer attend to the spiritual needs of some, neither can its sick club alleviate the financial needs of others. Even the subterranean toilets, which were kept in excellent condition by their attendants, had a most important part to play in life.

There is the memory of water seeping into the street from under the doors of the swimming baths, which was always accompanied by the shrieks and hollow-sounding pandemonium of the bathers inside. The fortunate ones possessed their very own costumes, which had ample coverage, leg room and sleeves. They were made of a cotton-type material, which either had a tendancy to cling affectionately to the body, displaying the manly figure of some, or, alternatively, to sag disastrously around the groin, giving one an uninspiring appearance.

You could, of course, hire a pair of "slips" for a penny. These white pocket handkerchief-size, almost transparent modest covering, would even be frowned on by some to-day. Thank God and the councillors that the last remaining dignified building, "The Library" still remains in situ, even though vandals make brainless attempts to destroy it.

Tuesdays was Gamuel Road School's day when books were changed. The bully boys then had the opportunity of crashing their books on the smaller boys heads with fiendish delight. I feel sure they chose the bulkiest volumes not for its reading content, but for sadistic purposes. We all gazed in rapt attention at the statue of Venus-de-Milo that stood in the same hall, some sniggered, some didn't. Whatever, we all admired it and wondered if a cleaner had accidently broken the arms when dusting it. Long may this great asset remain in its present form.

There were of course halls too numerous to mention by name. Perhaps the more well known was "The Druids Hall" and Walthamstow and Leyton Tram Depots. These were very popular. Most supplemented their income by being hired out for sixpenny and shilling hops. Some were used for spiritual guidance to those who hardly needed it, and to others, physical guidance, who had need when dancing. The tram depots were often promoting "Money Drives" and advertised prolific prizes of "Twenty Pounds Top" in gigantic letters. They were often spoiled by avaricious prize seekers who introduced deprecating remarks to the genuine whist lover who attended for its sociability and was only concerned in a pleasant game.

In time the timid type of person resigned from attending, leaving these spoilers to fight among themselves, while the rest enjoyed smaller drives with modest presents as prizes. On my one occasion when attending the "Money Drive" at Walthamstow Tram Depot, I was astounded during the interval by being accused of assisting my opponents to win, by one of these "prize hunters". He alleged as I had no chance myself, I was endeavouring to assist the opposing side to win. Fortunately, I was never a timid person, possibly careful to avoid unpleasantness, but certainly not timid. I cannot recall if this horrible specimen ever did "Get Lost".

The author, Mary Allen and her parents with family at Margate, 1926.

CHAPTER 13

An Imaginary Stroll in 1912

TO complete the nostalgic memories let us capture the atmosphere of a hot summer Saturday afternoon in 1912. We will meander from Bakers Arms to St James Street, with no desire to hurry. The activity and noise of the costermongers does little to drown the clang of the trams, where mysterious destinations appear high up on the top deck. The West Ham, brown fronted with a red diamond in the centre, in co-operation with the resplendent green Leyton Fleet, which sport curtains as an embellishment, are destined for the Docks. The sleek eight wheeled brown L.C.C. are bound for Bloomsbury, Liverpool Street and Aldgate.

Our own open deck "light railways" are decorated in bright red and cream and parked on the bend toward Whipps Cross. They are destined for the hazardous journey to Chingford, and are too near the stallholders for comfort. Whatever the colour, all trams have one thing in common, all the seats are of hard cane and tend to bruise one's bottom.

On the island, where the conveniences are discreetly placed underground, the newsboy vociferously announces the sale of "Westminster", "Pall Mall Gazette" and "Globe". Beside him sit the rubicund faced flower sellers, as philosophical in appearance as Buddha, and equally as colourful as their wares. At least three policeman are in evidence, with an ever watchful eye. In spite of the clamour a sense of orderliness prevails. On the forecourt of the public house itself horse brakes vie for hire, for trips to Epping Forest. "High Beach a Bob" is the familiar cry of the drivers, who later are to find opposition and eventually extinction, in the form of a fearsome new petrol driven invention "The Charabanc", generally called "sharabang". This was a high open coach bereft of shock absorbers, and mounted on solid tyres. The cobble stoned surface of Hoe Street is left behind, as we enter Boundary Road, a more quiet but dusty thoroughfare. An occasional breeze stirs the sandy surface which causes us to shade our eyes from the flying grit. Thankfully, a water cart appears, drawn by the well kept horse. The large tank of water serving the massive rear perforated bumper is making some effort in laying the dust and also causing the fragrant smell resulting from this action. The huge brick crushing plant in the builders yard also draws our attention and the wording on the open gates of "Goode Bros." reminds us of the present cinemas of Walthamstow built by them. "The Queens", "The Bell", "The Scala" is yet to be.

A train rumbles overhead, as we pass under the Midland Railway Bridge bound for Southend-on-Sea. Visions of this exciting town, with its salty air and its fivepenny cockle teas bring memories of the sea and its row of bathing machines, strictly separating the sexes. Why are they termed "Machines"? No mechanism is involved, apart from the old horse to pull them wherever required. Our thoughts are distracted by a gang of navvies, intent on making holes in the road. These weather beaten, formidable men all appear in a self imposed uniform. A thick red and blue striped Oxford shirt with a red handkerchief with white spots tied at the neck. Brown corduroy trousers, held up with a heavy leather belt, buckled dangerously near the navel. In general the stomachs overhang the belt, quite comfortably.

Two smaller straps are closely fitted below their knees, for what purpose? Is it for protection against rats when working in sewers or for ease in bending – or both? Four of them are engaged in swinging heavy sledge hammers following each other in perfect order. Their objective being of driving the chisel with intent of starting another hole. Their skill and accuracy, accompanied with the "Anvil chorus", is far more pleasing sound than the pneumatic drill of to-day. The hurricane lamps, both red and clear, are being filled with oil, at the side of the watchman's sentry box hut, where on a coke fired brazier a blackened kettle is steaming merrily – tea is on the way! This fire will be a welcome sight to the old watchman arriving later to protect the site against an almost unknown risk. "The Dotchies" fire mainly attracts children, drawn by its warmth and curiosity. Although the obstruction in the road is quite considerable there is no traffic hold-up. At present the two solitary cyclists, looked at us with some asperity, while impatiently ringing their bells, both considering our presence in the road unpardonable.

The appearance of "Richardsons" delivery van reminds me of an awful weal on my face, resulting in my foolish escapade in "whipping behind". The temptation to hang on the rear of vehicles was always present and on that occasion, I was lucky not to lose an eye. The driver had had expert practise in slashing his long corded whip, to the rear, as well as to the front. I never repeated that form of "whipping behind" again, although in later life, I was foolish enough to kneel on the bumper of a Walthamstow tram. By holding on to the projecting central lamp participated in the thrill of an hair raising ride, which on this occasion ended rather abruptly. It was during World War I, that the "conductress" neatly snatched my cap whilst I was looking sideways, showing off to my friends. The passengers rocked with merriment at the sight of me chasing the tram being appalled at the thought of returning home hatless! I was aghast. My weakness for this dangerous pastime was by now definitely and truly cured.

A Russian Jew, who had fled the pogroms of the Czar and raised his talented family in this country has a tailoring business on our right. Mr.

Goldberg, a fellow dabbler in gee-gees with father, greets us at his front door. His accent is as amusing as his stories are of Russia and the soldiers who persecuted him. They apparently eat nothing but sauerkraut "vich make them sheet und vort so terrible". This puzzles us for a while, but not his wife, who upbraids him unmercifully while looking skywards and requesting "Got vorgeeve heem".

The open acres of scrubland on our left, has not yet been exploited successfully by the speculative builder. We little realise this vast dump of old iron and general rubbish will be converted to allotments in a short two years. It was an exhausting task for the cultivators, who dug for victory in the cause to win "The war to end all wars". Now we have a clear view of Lea Bridge Road, where the LCC trams glide noiselessly, so far is the distance. Passing the Congregational Chapel, one of the many Sunday schools that I attended there is a terrace of Victorian cottages with extremely long front gardens, all well tended except for a few keeping a brood of fowls and one sporting a pigeon loft. The pigeon fancier is not very popular with the gardeners. No planning permission was needed for Mr Todd to convert his parlour into a barbers saloon. It was to this emporium I eagerly accompanied father on Sunday morning for his weekly shave and occasional snip of his wiry hair.

We carefully avoided tripping up, by treading gingerly on the well scuffed oil cloth, as we enter the narrow passage and turn left to view the scene. This haven was almost a club among the regular attenders. The smoke laden air to which father contributed in no small way, and the babble of conversation, which consisted of profane political discussions, interspersed with risque stories, was quite free of any foul language. I always made a bee line to the corner where back numbers of a tattered collection of comics and weeklys were in abundance. *Pearsons Weekly* and *Answers* were passed over in favour of *Chips, Butterfly, Funny Wonder, Jester, Comic Cuts, Chuckles*, whichever of these that were available. They all contained exciting interest and fun. As a diversion from the comics I was always fascinated by the operations of the master barber and his youthful assistant. The former, being a tall thin pale faced man, clean shaven, with a decided stoop, his balding head denied him the chance of recommending "Harlenes Hair Restorer". While sporting a long white coat, he proceeded to tie a none too clean towel to the front of his victim fully reclining in the chair, who was then subjected to the lathering by his assistant. Mr Todd then proceeded to complete his operation on the customer in the adjoining chair. The ceremony of honing the razor followed by the expert slapping on the shiny leather strop and the final application to the week old stubble of the customer. The rasping sound of the razor, travelling over the victims face, could almost be felt by the onlookers. I particularly was distracted from my perusal of "Weary Willie and tired

Tim", and winced at the sound. Next to the strop, stood a steaming kettle sitting on a gas ring being fed by a length of rubber tubing, attached to a gas bracket projecting from the wall. The young schoolboy assistant was never without a task, and when not occupied in lathering or sweeping the fallen hair into a convenient corner was cutting newspaper into 6" squares, and threading them on string. When first observing this, I imagined they were for the convenience of toilet hygiene, but no! They were placed on the shoulder of the customer, and used as a depository for used lather. After Sweeney Todd had skillfully flicked the lather into a much used sink, he would wipe the blade of the razor clean on the paper so conveniently placed. The patiently waiting clients would still be continuing the conversation of the highest order, the recent National Health Act by Lloyd George still came into criticism, or the latest murder. The latter always conjured up a morbid imagination, mainly because the felon always ended up with a hanging. This was considered by all a fitting climax, and gave satisfaction to many except the one at the end of the rope.

Eventually it would be father's turn as I catch the whiff of Mrs Barber's Sunday joint being prepared in the adjoining room. This aroma with the burning shag, beery breaths, and a faint smell of escaping gas, in this tight little room made a peculiar mixture. Having paid his 2d for the services rendered we leave the rendezvous to the cries of "So long George", that is now lost in time.

Crossing Chester Road, we observe a shop, which has passed now for ever. This is "Buckmasters", with its oil sodden, wooden floor, which houses a working bench, littered with nuts and bolts and other paraphenalia connected with his calling. "Mr Buckmaster"! A tolerant and genial personality, spends almost his entire life clad in a greasy blue boiler suit, tinkering with his mechanical stock. The window display of cycle pedals, bells etc, commands an undying interest. On the right of the shop is a collection of the most sorry sight of bedraggled cycles, for hire at the cost of 2d per hour. Within a few years of our stroll, I became one of the hapless hirers, to enjoy the opportunity of escaping to Whipps Cross, and careering up and down the sand hills, which had been left years before, from the gravel production. If one was fortunate enough to make the return journey unscathed, or without a broken chain, brake failure – or, most common of all, a puncture you would be extremely fortunate. The fish shop next, which attracts all at night with the tempting smell of its fried products mixed with hot chips and vinegar. This is such a contrast from the morning when the horrible aroma of gutted fish is being prepared for the evening trading with boxes of residue awaiting disposal. So we have one stop satisfying the adventurous spirit, another satisfying ones hunger, whilst further on the

"Duke of Cambridge" never satisfying the besotted wretches that frequented it.

Of all the public houses that I knew, this one held me with a peculiar fear. Its sawdust floor complete with spitoons, the doors open during summer days, the stale smell of beer and tobacco penetrating even the outside air. Its ox-like proprietor's strength was at times put to the test by ejecting brawling semi-intoxicated customers, who invariably completed their bout of fisticuffs on the Boundary Fields opposite. "Fight up the Cambridge" was a common enough cry to hear at quite regular intervals. This broadcast resulted in a concerted rush to the venue, to obtain a front line view of the bloody contestants, slogging each other. Of all the indescribable types who frequented this establishment, none were more revolting than the individual who would volunteer to bite a rat's head off for the price of a pint. He carried his stock in trade with him. I feel it was this facet that finally completed my detestation of this particular pub. On the opposite corner was another beer house, that absorbed the residue of those who had caused trouble in the former and larger drinking house. The fights and the obnoxious drunks finally finished up in utter ignomy and disgrace by being strapped on the police hand cart, which appeared eventually with two burly coppers, and trundled off to Lea Bridge Road Police Station. Remember, the police in those days were specially selected for their height and physical prowess, and no one dared to intervene. Law was Law.

Passing on, the next narrow turning, Markhouse Place, was definitely an isolated slum into which I never ventured at any time. It was here the family mentioned in the Gamuel Road School episode, resided, or rather existed. The end of this road terminated in what was known as "The Back Field". There were several places of waste land in this vicinity and all were used as playgrounds, or old iron depositories. Here the urchins had a peculiar hobby of digging large and deep holes in the hard baked earth, covering them with sacks and building fires in tins on the edge of the hole. They then proceeded to make cocoa filched from their respective houses, in actual fact emulating a form of Trogolytes.

The next two shops are Richardson's, previously mentioned in the scene of the "Great Bakers Robbery". Here oval dog biscuits were stolen in great numbers and distributed to whoever required them.

Beaconsfield Road is the next turning to observe in which I resided between the ages of one and six and has been described earlier. Next of course is Gamuel Road, housing the seat of learning, without which I would have been unable to pursue this narrative. Alexandra Road, the last of the turnings, has one particular character interest. A most peculiar little unique dairy set back from the road painted a vivid green with a flat counter over a small door on which a wind up bell is fitted. On pressing same, an old lady would emerge from the darkened interior and proceed to fill one's jug from a large milk can. I often wondered why she did not use the huge china bowl in the window on which a picture of a bonneted milk-maid is seated on a three legged stool, milking a placid and contented smiling cow, with a herd in the background. The words "Pure Milk" were imprinted above the picture. My thoughts were directed to who were the lucky persons to be served from this bowl, surmising of course that it contained a superior substance mentioned to that in the urn. However, now one considers how pure the milk was prior to pasturisation. We enter Markhouse Road, which has a written history, although few of the populace are aware.*

St. Saviours Church which nowadays we see stands out complete with a convent administering relief and succour to the very poor by the Sisters of Mercy. It also boasts a church school, which was at constant war with Gamuel Road Council School. This dominant church suffered the ravages of fire at one time, but has been restored almost to its usual splendour.

The first row of shops on the right incorporates the inevitable fried fish shop that revelled in the name of "The Dripping Shop" as all fish was fried in dripping which came in huge casks. My parents had dubious thoughts about the animal from which the dripping was extracted. With meaning glances horses were mentioned. However, we never purchased from that catering establishment, mainly because it lacked the usual aroma allied to shops of similar nature. Now we see a row of cottages similar to those in Boundary Road with extremely long front gardens, one or two carrying on business as jobbing builders or scrap merchants.

These were followed by another parade of shops which opened and closed with monotonous regularity excepting one in particular. This was a barbers owned by a German family, "Schmidts", who suffered the awful rioting which broke out during the First World War. Even in those days, there was an element of brainless vandals who took the opportunity of looting, under

---

*The Manor of Marks, once standing in this area was the property of the Priory of St. Helens, Bishopsgate, and the rents of this ecclesiastical property prior to Henry VIII' reign was £376.6d yearly. The Manor House was occupied by various ancient families and gave its name to Markhouse Lane, latterly to Markhouse Road. Thomas Nelson of Markhouse resided from 13.3.1799 to 16.5.1883 and concerned himself with the rights of Epping Forest. It is little known that, thanks to his perserverance and litigation, he played a large part in acquiring the Forest for the common man, by exposing unlawful enclosures of 3,000 acres, plus two ponds, and some waste land. For this and sundry beneficial acts he was knighted on 21.4.1880 at Windsor Castle by Queen Victoria, and subsequently died on 7th February 1885, and was buried at Teddington. This grand Manor was demolished in 1898, thus did Walthamstow lose one of its most historical houses. For further historical information I recommend Vestry House Museum.

the pretence of patriotism. I see even now the smashed fittings and wash basins actually torn from the walls and remember the sad sight of the family cowering in the back room of which the door had been wrenched off its hinges. They in turn were rescued eventually by the intervention of the stolid old English Bobby.

A similar occurrence happened in High Street to a German pork butcher, by the name of "Muckenfuss", this was often termed by some as "Muckingface" or other various names, assisted by the addition of further consonants, which can be left to your imagination. This type of behaviour was general in most districts where German immigrants were living and I suppose it was inevitable, especially as the propaganda used to stir the patriotic fervour was prolific. Posters of bayonetted babies by "The Huns" and paperback books of atrocities were many. "Murder Most Foul" was the title of one of these particular paper-backs that my parent caught me reading. This was hastily torn from my grasp and destroyed with the false idea of keeping the horrors from me, which proved quite fruitless.

Returning to our stroll we gaze at the Methodists unique chapel, known as "The Lighthouse", a veritable building deserving of that name. Built as its title suggests and whose beam circles from its tower, a beacon of goodwill and was only extinguished when the enemy made its initial air raids in the First World War. I, too, went to the Lighthouse Sunday School when the family moved to Byfield now Campus Road. During this war I have a clear recollection of "The Rev. Coll" or Cole, the preacher at the time, who exuded Christianity and was loved by all, especially the children. The P.S.A. "Pleasant Sunday Afternoon" was far in advance of its time with its recitals an attraction, enjoyed by many. Opposite this Christian edifice stands the "Common Gate" with a large sawdust floor taproom, interspersed with the usual iron spittoons. The open door exudes its fetid atmosphere which is in contrast to the wholesome smell of newly baked bread from the bakers known as "Sextons" on the opposite corner. It is worthy to note the Lighthouse still stands and is operational whilst the "Common Gate" has only just reopened after being closed many years and is known as The Sportsman.

Dunbars the chemist was the only pharmacy in the area and was bravely kept in business by a chronic arthritic, a Mr. Dunbar, whose counter was all of three feet square, from which he served his drugs. The rest of the shop was taken up by the dispensary and stock obscured by high glass display cabinet.

The butchers opposite Dunbars are great friends, Mr & Mrs Westley being the proprietors. Mr Westley, a kindly cadaverous tall man with a sweeping Saxon moustache, was a true butcher garbed in a long rough blue coat over which was tied the popular blue and white striped apron. He had graduated from Smithfields and actually bought his cattle at Romford and with assistance drove them to the slaughter house in Hoe Street. He then killed and skinned and prepared his merchandise for public consumption. His wife, a jolly, rosy cheeked, dark haired Irish colleen of ample proportions, whose generosity was almost a fault, while the gambling habit of her husband definitely were. In later years, party's given by this delightful couple were a great success enhanced by three attractive daughters.

On one occasion the usual "knees up" dance caused part of the shop ceiling to fall and distribute itself over our breakfast prepared sausages. Fortunately the meat was away in the cold store, kept at freezing temperature by one hundred weight blocks of ice supplied by the United North Pole Ice Co. Delivery of these were made by horsedrawn carts, and carried in on the shoulders of burly carters, the ice being wrapped in soaking sacks and pulled from the cart by vicious looking hooks. Urchins would gather to purloin pieces of broken ice to suck with evident enjoyment "such taste" when one is young. However, as my calling was a plasterer, it behove of me to repair the damage. For this I was pressed to accept half-a-crown for the work in question, such was his nature, even though I had assisted in the cause of the catastrophe.

Our interest is taken by the last two shops before Ringwood Road. One sells gramophones, while the corner one is "Claydens". This unique dairy had their own cows which were kept in the field opposite, and milked in the shed in the mews at the rear of the shop by Mr. Clayden. He, also, is another immense dark man with an equally large black moustache. His windows displayed polished milk cans and china swans carrying an array of eggs between their resplendent wings. At the end of the marble counter is a well constructed trellis work holding "Nevill's Bread". This unique flour bedecked "Coburg" loaf with a quality of its own, baked in steam ovens, possesses a tempting and delicious appearance with a compensating flavour. There is no equivalent of this unique loaf today. The tinny-strains of "Ragtime Cowboy Jo" or "Alexanders Ragtime Band" can be heard from the shop next door being relayed from the recently improved horn gramophone, embellished in a variety of colours. On the opposite corner stands "Watsons Lino Emporium", displaying a huge notice stating "No connection with the shop next door". The offending shop in question was one trading in the same merchandise. The stock here was of such a meagre variety that I am sure Watsons need not have been unduly concerned by the opposition as at most times all one saw was a meagre stock of lino. This was mainly used to obscure a regular card school from the prying eyes of the law. A short distance from Searls on the opposite side one can see across a large enclosed meadow, on

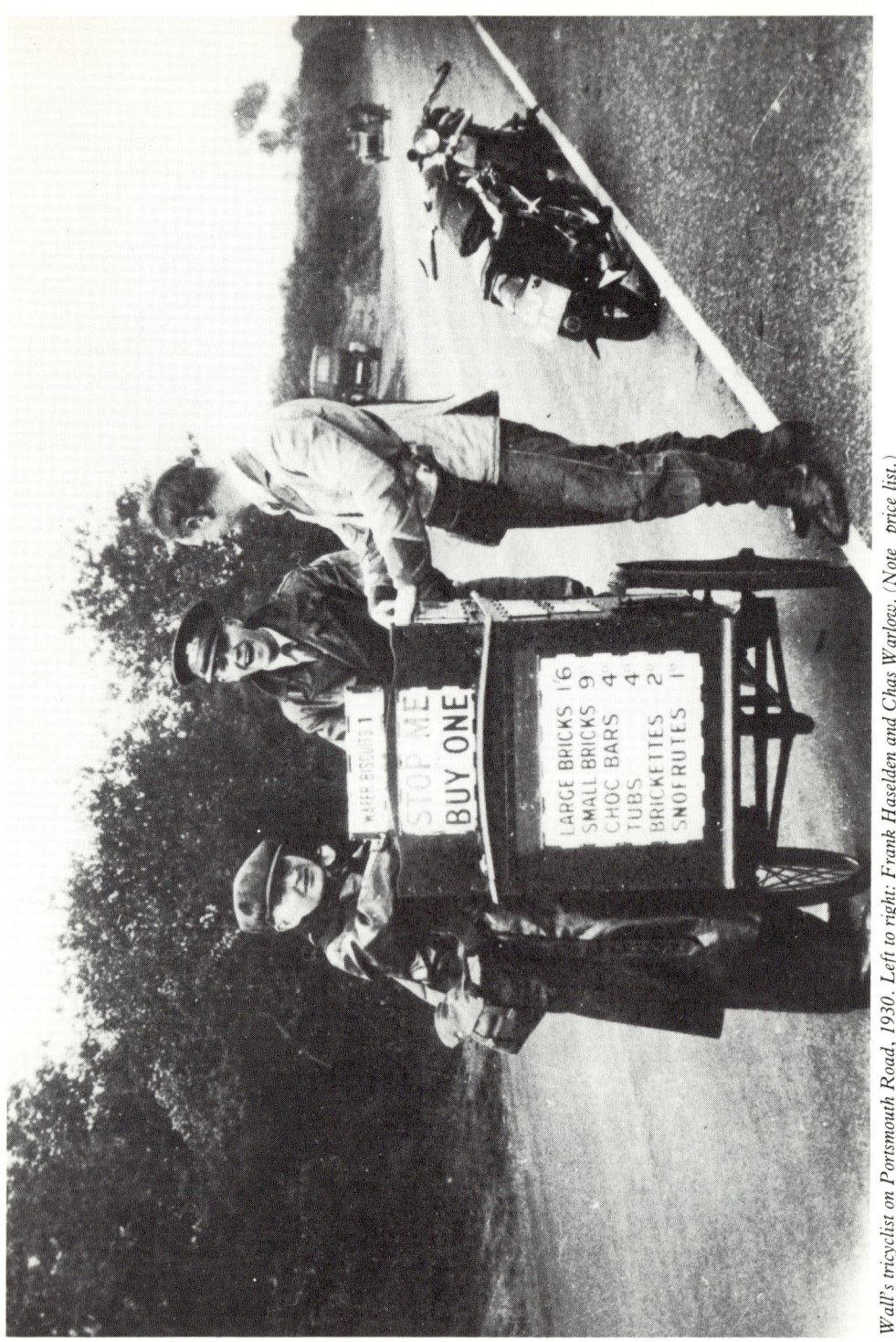

Wall's tricyclist on Portsmouth Road, 1930. Left to right: Frank Haselden and Chas Warlow. (Note price list.)

which the cows of Claydens Dairy contentedly graze and stare with typical curiosity at the trams that clank on their way to Higham Hill.

Further on we approach a distinguished house on the corner of Camden Road, bearing a highly polished brass plate on which was inscribed Dr. Moore M.D. Hours 9-11 and 6-7.30. This we regard with great respect and carefully remove our headgear should we enter his waiting room for medical attention.

The most unique shop next of note is Strutts. This extremely old Walthamstow family have handed down their skills of sweet making for many generations – They are most famous for various flavoured rocks, coconut candy and ice, manufactured on the premises. All of their products are deliciously pure, and cut up by a fearsome pair of pincers, or broken by an all steel hammer. Mrs Strutt a buxom pleasant-faced lady presides over brass bowled scales that are thickly lined with residue of the sweetmeats. Although the scales were always tipped in favour of the purchaser, they would not have passed official inspection.

We may gaze in Reads newsagent opposite for a short period to absorb the adventures of the comic characters portrayed on the front pages of the *Firefly, Rainbow* and *Puck* which among others are hung up in the side window, with the object of enticing one to buy and enjoy a further feast of clean fun.

I trust you will not object to crossing the road once again, making sure that you are not run over by "Prices" horse-drawn bread van, in which the driver is vainly endeavouring to free the thinly steel shod wheels, which have been caught in the tram lines. The van is being dragged at a rather dangerous angle by a somewhat scared horse experiencing the painful end of the whip being used rather unnecessarily.

Here is "Lankshears", the "in and out shop", which is actually a pawn shop. The title has two origins, one, the pawning operation – "In and out", the second the whole front was wide open, enabling a person to enter and leave at will. They also deal in rough working clothes, hob nailed boots, Oxford shirts, aprons etc. Next door is a mysterious shuttered premises, bearing no sign for its purpose. Its only entrance is in a dimly lit side passage. It is known as "The Club", a low drinking den of iniquity. As a child I looked upon it with fear, mainly as a result of mother's abhorence and veiled remarks, which may have been because it was strictly "men only", and appeared to hold hidden and secretive activities.

However, did you notice the small corrugated iron building known as the South Grove Mission Hall whose principal was the Rev. Mr. Robbins. It is situated just before Lankshears and lays well back from the main road. In fact it has a secondary entrance in Arkley Road at the rear. Here again I was occasionally "ordered" to attend on summer Sunday evenings with two of my cronies, to assist in swelling the dwindling congregation. The choir was extremely vociferous and excellent in quality. Two of my sisters, Winnie and May, were regular members who not only enjoyed the hymns taken from "Gospel Bells" but also were attracted to and by the opposite sex. This particular choir sat on a rather high platform surrounded by a wooden rail, very reminiscent of the type seen in Madam Tusauds Chamber of Horrors, whereon the felons all stand against the background of the gallows. I hasten to add this remarkable resemblance is in no way meant in a derogatory manner, or to even suggest the choir had any relationship to the Victorian and Edwardian criminals. It was only the plain and cold looking platform high and aloof from the audience, that struck me as unique and peculiar.

Below this platform sat Mr. Robbins, an immaculately dressed, white haired bearded man, facing his worshippers, crossed legged with an evangelical smile to all. Just behind him was the organist, whose solemnity was only surpassed by his rendition of Handels Largo with variations. It will be noticed to-day this little Christian oasis has been re-built and refurbished beyond recognition, by another denomination of a more forceful and persistant character. Often after Sunday Evensong the enthusiastic ones would bring a little harmonium out into Arkley Crescent at the rear, which was by no means the select of roads, and proceed to sing the praises, of the Lord and inviting sinners to repent. Such was the fervour which I witnessed, not fully understanding the whole matter of approach.

We are nearing the end of Markhouse Road. A few more steps will give us the opportunity to look into "Kendals Gown and Mantle Shop" displaying the latest models with hobble skirts and braided costumes. The high necked lace blouses are surmounted by atrociously large hats, some displaying doves in full flight, and others resembling a small flower patch, interlaced with artificial mouth watering cherries. The price of these articles were far beyond many pockets. "Fancy paying 19/11d for that costume?"

Almost next door and the last building in Markhouse Road opposite the "Brewery Tap' public house stands the large construction of the Essex Club, later to become Sherry's Billiard Hall, whose dark interior was not conducive or inviting. I have no doubt the minor criminals and tearabouts found it an ideal rendezvous for the hatching of plots criminal or otherwise. The centre of the road you may find convenient – it is an underground convenience – now demolished.

I invite you to meet me here shortly, as I would like to continue our stroll and my story along other thoroughfares. BYE BYE!

CONCLUSION

The period from 1906-1930 has been portrayed quite simply as I have fared while it lasted.

Its politics and past councils have been omitted, although I have memories of some colourful representatives, namely Pemberton Billing, a most flamboyant character, and latterly Mr. McEntee of whom father boasted rather disparagingly "I knew him when he was a carpenter". This I thought was more to Mr. McEntee's credit.

The local administration has progressed by somewhat different methods than those at the turn of the century. To confirm this, I respectfully quote from the comments printed in the "Daily Graphic" in 1902, under "Wild Walthamstow" – "Those who like their politics hot, should go to Walthamstow". Fights in the local chamber were frequent. Personal abuse was commonplace – reporters were barred from meetings – members were liable to be called to order by a blow on the head from the gavel – whilst debates could be closed by the knocking out of teeth etc.

Thank goodness we have passed this Dickensian type of Government – or have we?

Looking at the problems of to-day, which increase in variance by the hour, I consider the much maligned councillors need assistance from the public quite as much as the public needs from them. I considered Walthamstow in the period covered, as an overgrown village, gradually losing both its character and characters. I therefore sincerely hope I have kept alive, on paper, a few of the latter worthy of memory. On this note I close this episode of my life in the anticipation of continuing further reminiscences in the dim and distant future, which at present is obscure although the past is exceptionally clear.